It is hard today to imagine the way people lived a thousand years ago. At that time Europe was dominated by one force—religion—and the focus for all religious people was Jerusalem.

For as long as history has been recorded, the city has been a religious center. Taken by King David in about 1000 BC, it became the Hebrews' capital. It was there that David's son, Solomon, built the First Temple and King Herod rebuilt the Second Temple—the centers of Jewish religious life. To Christians, Jerusalem is filled with reminders of the New Testament and the life of Jesus Christ: it was the city He entered in triumph, Golgotha the place where He was crucified. Muslims captured Jerusalem in the year 637 and built a great mosque there, called the Dome of the Rock. Muslim tradition marks Jerusalem as the place where the Prophet Mohammed ascended to heaven.

Inevitably, the city came to be seen as a glittering prize in a Europe aflame with religious passion. On November 27, 1095, Pope Urban II issued a call to arms—"Deus lo volt!" (God wills it!)—and the first Crusade was launched. The Crusaders united in massive armies and marched into Asia, spreading terror along their route, with the purpose of reclaiming the Holy Land from the Muslims. The first century of the millennium ended with the bloody conquest of Jerusalem by the knights of the First Crusade.

A A PEACEFUL CRUSADE
A pilgrimage is nothing less than a peaceful crusade, and throughout history cities with religious shrines have been magnets for pilgrims. This is a sculpture of St. James in the traditional garb of a medieval pilgrim: walking staff, wide-brimmed hat, and seashell badge. A person dressed in this fashion would be relatively safe from robbery or harassment on the main roads of Europe.

B CONSTANTINOPLE The largest city in medieval Europe, it was dominated by the Hagia Sophia, the Great Church of the Emperor Justinian. Triple walls enclosed a metropolis of more than 250,000 people, more than four times the population of Rome.

1 CLERMONT-FERRAND, NOVEMBER 27, 1095 Pope Urban II issued his call to arms in this French village. The first army, of over twenty thousand peasants led by a religious zealot called Peter the Hermit, who dressed like a monk and rode a donkey, left in the spring. It was soon followed by two professional Crusader armies of knights on horseback supported by foot soldiers.

2 COLOGNE, MAY–JUNE 1096 Filled with the fever of righteousness, a German contingent of Crusaders turned into an uncontrollable mob here, robbing and murdering Jews in towns along the Rhine.

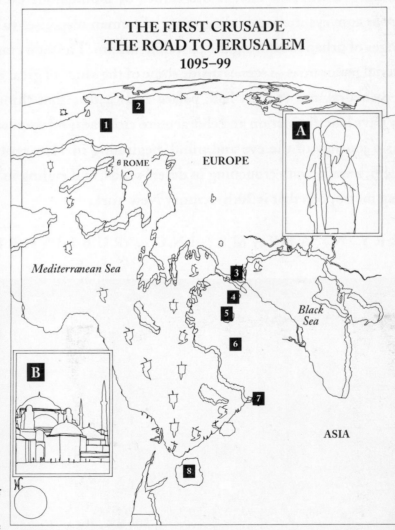

THE FIRST CRUSADE
THE ROAD TO JERUSALEM
1095–99

EUROPE
ROME
Mediterranean Sea
Black Sea
ASIA

3 CONSTANTINOPLE, 1097 The Crusader army assembled here before proceeding to Jerusalem. By the middle of the year, there were almost seventy thousand Crusaders before the city walls. Concerned that the horde might turn on his city, Emperor Alexius had them ferried across the Bosporus, into Asia.

4 CIVETOT, OCTOBER 21, 1096 Peter the Hermit's army of men, women, and children traveled in advance of the army of knights and foot soldiers. On this day they were surrounded by the Turks, and a slaughter ensued. This was the end of the People's Crusade. Peter escaped.

5 NICAEA, JUNE 19, 1097 The Crusaders' first important military objective in Asia was Nicaea. Hoping to starve the defenders into submission, the Crusaders laid siege to the town, which fell on this day.

6 DORYLAEUM, JULY 1, 1097 Although they suffered heavy casualties, the Crusaders prevailed over the Turks in this huge battle.

7 ANTIOCH, JUNE 3, 1098 This city, which controlled the busy route from Asia into Syria and Jerusalem, fell to the Crusaders by treachery.

8 JERUSALEM, JUNE 7, 1099 The Crusaders stood at the city walls.

To the Holy Land

1000
IN CHINA
Gunpowder
perfected

1003
THE NEW WORLD
Leif Eriksson lands
in Newfoundland

1013
FAMED
MOSQUE
Al Hakim,
Cairo

1019
PEACE
Canute king of
England and
Denmark

1097
SCOURGE
STRIKES
Plague kills
100,000

1094
ON THE
CANALS
Gondolas in
Venice

1091
HEAVENLY
MYSTERY
Lunar eclipse
seen in Italy

1088
TELLING
TIME
Astronomical
clock, China

1086
DAY OF
JUDGMENT
Domesday cen-
sus, England

1085
KINGS OF THE
NORTH
Eskimos across
North America

1071
TO THE EAST
African ports
send ambassadors
to China

1067
TOWER OF
LONDON
Construction
begins

A CITY BESIEGED

On June 7, 1099, the Crusaders gathered on a hill overlooking Jerusalem, a city poised between East and West and desert and sea, peopled by Muslims, Jews, and Christians of numerous sects, all living in relative harmony among the sacred shrines of their respective faiths. After one assault was repelled on June 13, the Crusaders began to build wheeled wooden towers equipped with catapults. With these they took Jerusalem on July 15, slaughtering many of the city's citizens, including virtually all of the Muslims.

1036
DISASTER
Earthquake
in China kills
23,000

1037
MUSLIM
SCHOLAR
Ibn Sina dies

1042
ON PRESS
Movable-
type printing,
China

1044
INNOVATION
First "float-
ing" compass,
China

1066
SAXONS LOSE
Norman victory
at the Battle of
Hastings

1053
CATHEDRAL
Construction
begins, Pisa

1050
BEFORE THE
SEXTANT
First astrolabes
in Europe

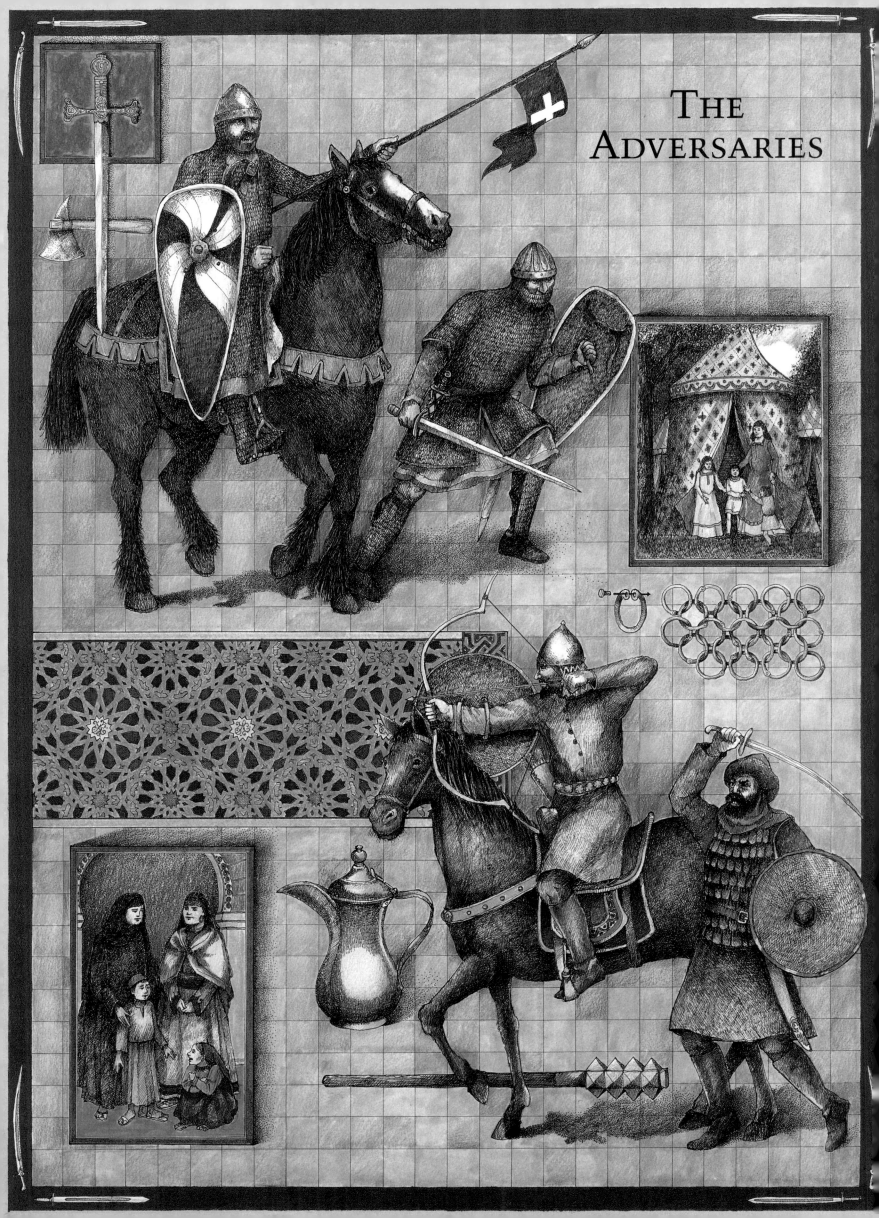

THE
ADVERSARIES

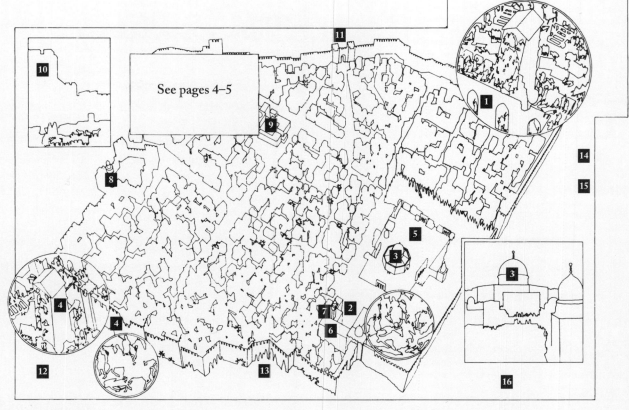

1 HEROD'S GATE The Crusaders moved their siege towers into position near Herod's Gate on July 15. The Muslims bombarded them with Greek fire (a substance similar to napalm), arrows, spears, and stones, but they were overwhelmed.

2 AL AQSA MOSQUE The defenders were swept back into the area of the Dome of the Rock and Al Aqsa Mosque. It was here that the greatest slaughter of the Muslim defenders took place.

3 DOME OF THE ROCK This mosque, completed in the year 691, has changed little since 1099. With its gold-covered dome, it is one of the world's finest examples of Muslim architecture.

4 ZION GATE The Crusaders also breached the city wall near here.

5 TEMPLE MOUNT The Crusaders moved in from the west.

6 KING HEROD'S SECOND TEMPLE The temple, built here in the first century AD, had massive supporting walls made of huge blocks—including the Wailing Wall.

7 WAILING WALL Judaism's most holy site.

8 TOWER OF DAVID The governor of Jerusalem surrendered the tower to the Crusaders in exchange for safe passage out of the city. The tower had been built on the site of one of three great defensive towers constructed during the reign of King Herod.

9 HOLY SEPULCHRE The most sacred shrine in Jerusalem to the Crusaders. The first Church of the Holy Sepulchre was built here after 326, when it was determined to be the site of Christ's tomb.

10 JAFFA GATE The most prominent architectural element in the western facade of the old city wall.

11 DAMASCUS GATE The most impressive gate to the old city. The trade route to Damascus started here.

12 MOUNT ZION

13 DUNG GATE

14 TOMB OF THE VIRGIN Inside the underground Church of the Assumption.

15 GARDEN OF GETHSEMANE Where Jesus and his disciples went after the Last Supper. The name comes from the words meaning "oil press," a reference to the olive trees that were once abundant here.

16 MOUNT OF OLIVES The site of the oldest cemetery still in use, where Jews have been buried for two thousand years.

1 CRUSADER FAMILY

2 ISLAMIC MOSAICS

3 MUSLIM FAMILY

4 CRUSADER KNIGHT He wore chain mail to protect himself. Because his armor and weapons weighed so much, a knight had to have at least two horses. The one ridden in battle was big and heavy; a smaller horse carried him over distances. He carried a lance and battle-ax as well as a sword that usually contained a holy relic in its knob.

5 CHAIN MAIL This type of lightweight, flexible protection is probably of Persian or Chinese origin.

6 MUSLIM HORSEMAN He rode an extremely fast Arabian steed. As a result, the Muslim army was much more mobile than the Crusader army. Muslim weapons—a small bow that could be used from horseback and a sword made of steel—were designed to be light.

Paris, 12th century

Though some call them the Dark Ages, this description of the Middle Ages, a thousand-year-long period, couldn't be more misleading—especially when referring to the 12th century. This was a time of learning and the birth of many great universities; of the breakdown of feudalism and the growth of the city; of increased trade and the rise of the middle class. Of course, the Church was still extremely powerful, for it gave a structure and a meaning to everyday life: the hope of eternal bliss.

With society's increased wealth, there was suddenly a huge building boom in the cities and towns, especially in Paris and other bishops' seats, or *cathedra*. In mid-century, a new crusade was launched in many great European cities—some call it the "cathedral crusade"—focusing on building enormous, gloriously decorated, soaring structures that made the most of the new Gothic style. Gothic architecture glorified both God and His human subjects (especially, it was hoped, those who helped finance the hugely expensive projects). The drive to build was mind-boggling: between 1170 and 1270 the French alone built eighty cathedrals.

Today, Paris is one of the greatest cities in the world, but it had humble beginnings. In 52 BC Julius Caesar's troops conquered a small fishing village on the Seine River. Originally inhabited by members of a Gallic tribe called the Parisii, the settlement eventually took on its founders' name. The Romans found a druid sanctuary there and, seizing this sacred space, constructed a temple of their own on the same site. Later, Christians built a basilica over its ruins—the place of worship was called "Our Lady" as early as the 6th century—and then in 1163 Pope Alexander III laid the cornerstone there for one of the most exquisite architectural achievements of history, the Cathedral of Notre-Dame.

THE RISE OF THE CATHEDRAL 1163–14TH CENTURY

A CATHEDRAL OF NOTRE-DAME (CATHEDRAL OF OUR LADY) In a huge wave of philanthropy, throngs of people, from the king—whose seat was in Paris—to serfs, donated money to Bishop Maurice de Sully's campaign to build Notre-Dame. Even in the 12th century, Paris was an important site. It enjoyed many of the benefits of a prime piece of real estate: a location near many rivers (which meant easy transportation), extremely fertile surroundings, and abundant supplies of building materials (high-quality granite and limestone) nearby.

B ILE DE LA CITÉ (CITY ISLAND) Notre-Dame is at the eastern end of the island upon which Paris was born. Some sense of medieval life can still be gleaned from its crooked streets crowded by three- and four-story houses. In the 12th century, the streets were crammed with travelers from a multitude of lands speaking dozens of languages. They all had to step carefully to prevent collisions with each other and with oxcarts, but also to avoid the rivers of waste flowing in the streets—all refuse was simply thrown out the window in these days before indoor plumbing.

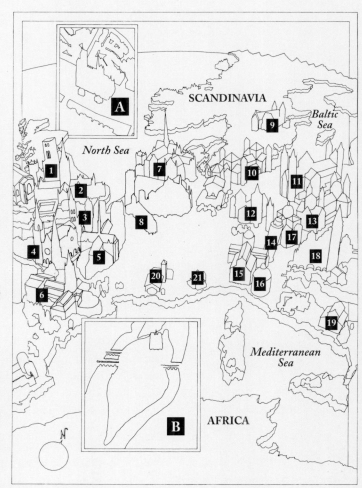

1 DURHAM CATHEDRAL
2 SALISBURY CATHEDRAL The original cathedral was built on a windy hilltop, so windy that the howling interfered with saying mass.
3 ST.-DENIS CATHEDRAL This is Europe's first Gothic structure.
4 CHARTRES CATHEDRAL
5 NOTRE-DAME CATHEDRAL
6 ST.-SERNIN CATHEDRAL, TOULOUSE
7 AMIENS CATHEDRAL
8 BOURGES CATHEDRAL
9 LUND CATHEDRAL
10 ST. MICHAEL'S CATHEDRAL, HILDESHEIM
11 WORMS CATHEDRAL
12 TRIER CATHEDRAL The seamless robe of Jesus—the "Holy Coat of Trier"—resides here.
13 SPEYER CATHEDRAL
14 CAMPANILE, PISA
15 PISA CATHEDRAL
16 BAPTISTRY, PISA
17 PARMA CATHEDRAL
18 ST. MARK'S CATHEDRAL, VENICE The building has five domes.
19 SAN MINIATO CATHEDRAL
20 ST.-GILLES-DU-GARD CATHEDRAL
21 ST.-HILAIRE CATHEDRAL, POITIERS

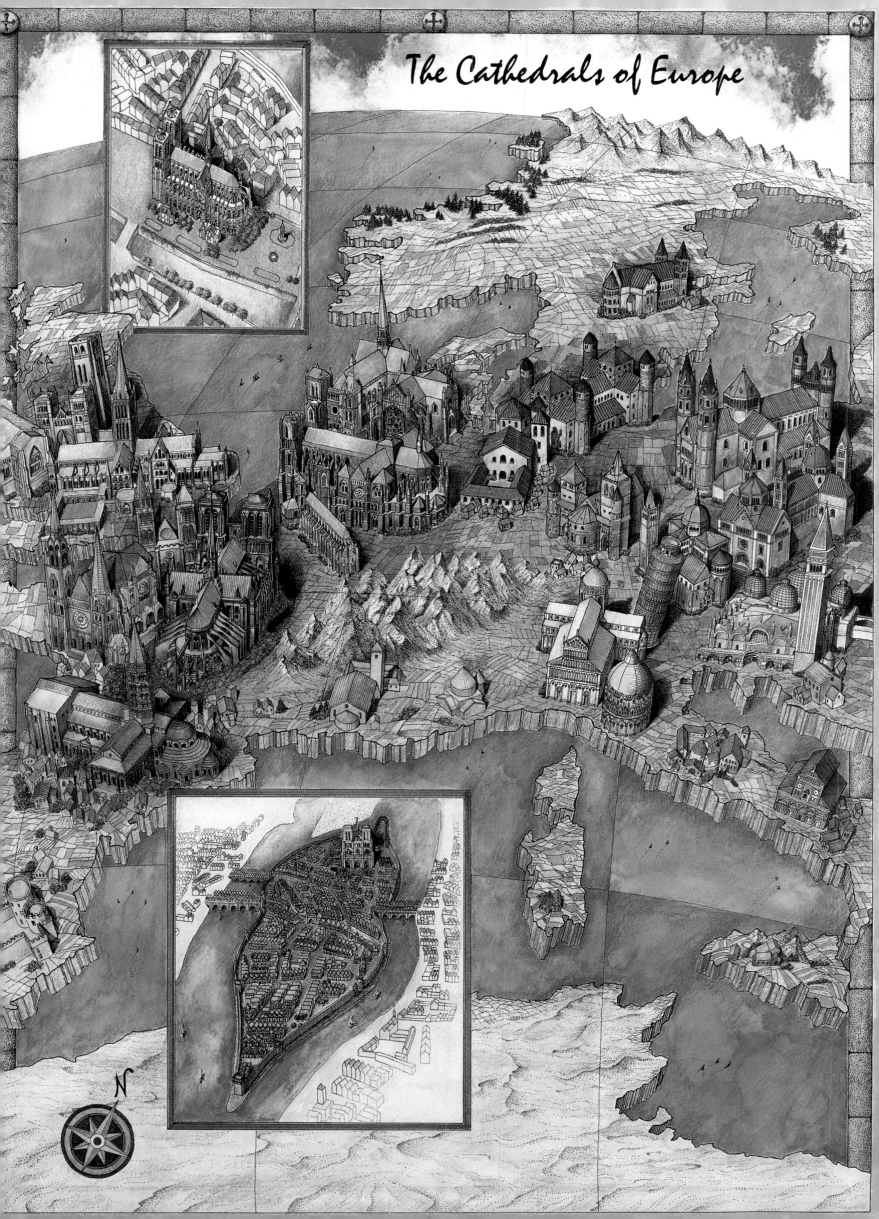

The Cathedrals of Europe

How to Build a Cathedral

The first step was to dig a huge hole for the building's foundations, which would contain millions of tons of stone. (Often, once a cathedral was completed as above.) Then a series of specialized professionals arrived to do their jobs. They all worked in an environment tightly controlled by the guilds, early versions of today's labor unions.

Today, Notre-Dame is so quiet that a loud voice turns heads. But how noisy it must have been in the late 12th century with hammers pounding, smiths' anvils clanging, workmen shouting, and carts rumbling!

1100
SLINGSHOT
The trebuchet
in general use

1113
ONION
DOMES
St. Nicolas
Novgorod
founded

1120
A NEW
DEAL
Playing cards
invented in
China

1123
RUBAIYAT
Persian
scientist and
poet Omar
Khayyam dies

1193
OUT OF INDIA
British import
indigo to use
as a dye

1192
RULER OF ALL JAPAN
Yoritomo Minamoto
becomes first shogun

1189
NEW ENGLISH KING
Richard the Lion-
Hearted crowned

1187
MUSLIM HERO!
Saladin takes
Jerusalem

1180
ROOM WITH
A VIEW
Glass windows
in English
homes

1179
MAYAN
RUINS
Chichén Itzá
sacked

1176
BUILD IT UP
London
Bridge
rebuilt of
stone, with
houses lining
each side

1174
IN PISA
Tower con-
struction
begins

1125
TRAVELING
MUSICIAN
Troubadours
arrive in
France

1139
THOU SHALT
NOT
Lateran
Council bans
crossbows

1145
CELESTIAL
VISITATION
Halley's
Comet
appears

1150
THE LARGEST
TEMPLE
Angkor Wat
completed

1151
CHECKMATE,
MATE
Chess arrives
in England

1155
MONGOL
LEADER
Genghis
Khan born

1158
SALT TRADE
Now based in
Munich

1170
DEATH OF A
SAINT
Thomas à
Becket
murdered

1167
CAIRO FALLS
King of
Jerusalem
takes the city

1161
BIG BANG
Explosives
used in battle,
China

1 QUARRYMEN AND LABORERS
Every single piece of stone for every cathedral built was quarried by hand; there were no explosives and no mechanical saws. Once out of the ground, the stone would be transported on barges or carts pulled by oxen or, often, men. Building each cathedral meant thousands upon thousands of trips—terribly (and sometimes fatally) hard labor, done by men with no hope of ever attaining any higher level of responsibility. Tensions often erupted in fistfights, which provided a welcome excuse for the onlookers to take a break.

2 MASONS The stone took on its final form on site. The mason doing the work was careful to cut a mark into it that would describe its final position. He also carved his own initials into each block, as he was paid by the piece. Some of these marks are still visible today.

3 SMITH Since cutting into stone dulls even the keenest iron blade very quickly, smiths had to sharpen chisels, saws, and other tools and forge new ones. Smiths also made chains used to hoist heavy materials.

See pages 10–11

6 MASTER GLASSMAKER One of the most dramatic aspects of the Gothic cathedral was the intense jewellike colors of the sunlight as it poured through the stained-glass windows. The glassmaker would add various chemicals to the molten glass to achieve this brilliant rainbow: cobalt for blue, silver oxide for yellow, iron oxide for red, and so on.

7 APPRENTICES The guild system was tightly controlled—a boy would start as an apprentice, not becoming a journeyman until he had completed years of boring, dangerous, and often backbreaking work.

8 FALSEWORK There was always a lot of suspense when the falsework—the collapsible woodwork supporting the stone arches during construction—was removed. If it came down before the mortar was sufficiently dry, the whole arch could fall. But if it was removed too late, the mortar would be too hard to allow the stones to settle, not permitting the strongest possible construction. When completely dry, the mortar—a combination of lime, water, and sand—was as strong as cement.

4 CARPENTER Anything made of wood—scaffolding, ladders, ramps, beams—was the responsibility of the carpenter. Finding enough wood for the job became increasingly difficult by the end of the 12th century, due to the amount of construction going on and frequent fires.

5 MASTER MASON The master of the works, or master mason, was a regal figure, in charge of everything from the architecture to every element of construction. He strode around the site in his elegant robes, carrying—but never wearing—a pair of gloves, a symbol that though he was in fact a mason by training, he now worked with his head, not his hands. Masters of the works were highly educated, intimidating figures.

9 GREAT WHEEL This machine was used to lift heavy loads. It was sometimes operated by a "human engine," a man walking or running endlessly on a treadmill.

10 ROOF Lead, slate, or tiles covered the wooden roof, to make it waterproof and more durable.

11 SCAFFOLDING The carpenter constructed a variety of temporary platforms for the workers to stand on. Some scaffolds were made of boards laid on other horizontal boards stuck into special holes in the walls, called pigeonholes. These holes can be seen today.

---

1 GARGOYLES When Notre-Dame was dedicated, all evil was said to be driven out of the cathedral. The dark powers were represented by the monsters known as gargoyles, who were all banished to the outside walls. There they also serve to direct the runoff rain and decorate the building's exterior in a dramatic fashion.

2 SCULPTURE This piece of exterior sculpture —one of about 1200—is meant to depict the horrors of hell, with souls twisted and writhing in torment. It served as a warning to Parisians: Worship and support your cathedral . . . or else!

3 STONE-CUTTING TOOLS Picks and axes helped reduce the enormous pieces of stone from the quarry into the precisely fitting blocks needed to build the cathedral. Masons used hammers and chisels for the more delicate work.

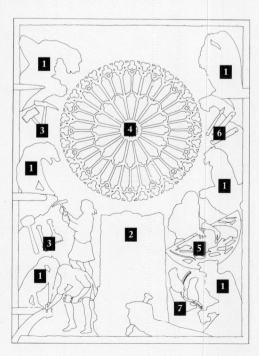

4 ROSE WINDOW This glorious window design was introduced in 12th-century France. The source of the name is obvious: each section radiates out from the center as petals do on a flower. Notre-Dame's north rose window survives intact from 1255.

5 STAINED GLASS In Gothic cathedrals the colored light it cast was seen as a manifestation of divine light.

6 STAINED-GLASS TOOLS Grozing irons (right) bit at and dividing irons (left) cracked the glass into shape.

7 COMPLETING THE WINDOW After cutting the glass into the chosen shapes, the artisan carefully bent lead to frame each piece and hold it in place.

In no other era, in no other place, has there ever been a time like this. This was the age dominated by a Mongol man named Temuchin (1155–1227)—better known as Genghis Khan, the leader of the greatest conquering army in history. Growing up in a nomadic culture on the Mongolian steppes, Temuchin learned to ride and hunt fearlessly at a young age. As suspicious of outsiders as he was loyal and generous to his friends, he impressed all who met him with his ferocity, determination, and charisma.

By the time he was in his forties, Temuchin had seized the reins of power, subdued all rivals, and unified Mongolia under his rule. Given the title Genghis Khan (Universal Leader) in 1206, he soon turned his sights outward, first south and then east to China, even breaking through the Great Wall of China. A Chinese writer of the time exclaimed, "Since the beginning of the world, no nation has been as powerful as these Mongols are now. They annihilate empires as if they were tearing up grass."

Next, the Mongols focused on the west. By the end of the century, their empire had reached proportions that are hard to believe—it stretched from the Pacific west to the Danube and from Lake Baikal south to the Persian Gulf.

A THE INVASION OF ASIA Mongol troops broke through the Great Wall and moved into China in 1211, capturing Peking four years later. Many Chinese joined Genghis Khan's forces after seeing their great power—and after he said that resistance would mean universal massacre. But before this campaign was complete, Genghis Khan had already turned his attention to the west, to Persia and beyond. His troops attacked at night, moving steadily and ruthlessly. By the time he had conquered these Muslim lands, 80% of the population of the Arabic-Iranic civilization was eradicated. After the conquered towns and cities were burned, the region began to resemble a steppe—just like home for the Mongols.

1 Lake Baikal
2 Mongolia
3 Peking
4 Samarkand
5 Black Sea
6 Persian Gulf

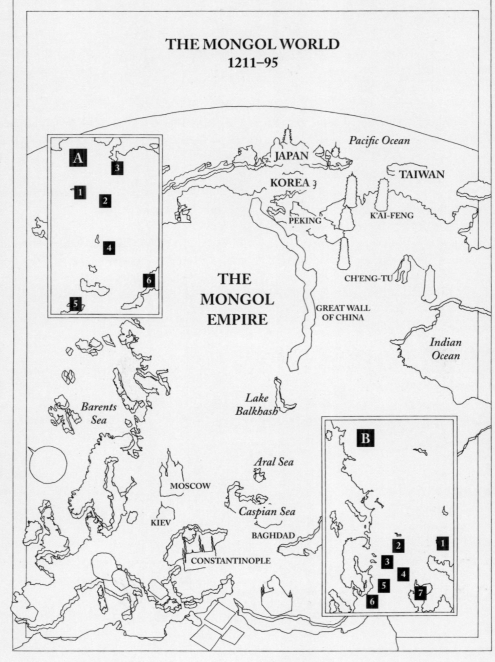

THE MONGOL WORLD
1211–95

THE MONGOL EMPIRE

Pacific Ocean
JAPAN
KOREA
TAIWAN
PEKING
K'AI-FENG
CH'ENG-TU
GREAT WALL OF CHINA
Indian Ocean
Barents Sea
Lake Balkhash
Aral Sea
MOSCOW
Caspian Sea
KIEV
BAGHDAD
CONSTANTINOPLE

B THE INVASION OF RUSSIA AND EASTERN EUROPE In 1237–40 the Mongols invaded Russia, destroying all but two of its cities. Then they moved on through Europe. Poised to enter Germany and France, they were forced to withdraw in 1242, when their leader died. The Mongols were extremely hardy and frugal. One traveler noted, "Neither cold nor heat, neither the long day's marches nor the discomforts of the journey over rocks, marshes, and raging streams, neither hunger nor thirst seemed to make the least impression on them. Never was there a complaint, or a word of reproach or a rebellious muttering, but always the same unruffled calm, the same cheerful mood, the same willing attitude."

1 Aral Sea
2 Bulgar
3 Moscow
4 Kiev
5 Krakow
6 Vienna
7 Black Sea

THE ENORMOUS EMPIRE

1200
PERU'S POWER
Manco Capac
founds Inca dynasty

1202
SMILES AND LAUGHTER
The first court jesters

1209
ORDER'S ORDERS
Franciscans' first rules

1212
CHILDREN'S C
Children set ou
the Holy Land

1296
IN FLORENCE
Sta. Maria
del Fiore
begun

1295
JOURNEYER RETURNS
Marco Polo
back to Italy

1291
CRUSADES END
Muslims capture Acre, the last Christian stronghold in Syria

1290
IN FOCUS
Spectacles
introduced in
Europe

A MOVABLE CITY

With their nomadic tradition—for generations, Mongols followed their herds on a seasonal migration through grazing lands—they adapted easily to their new itinerant military lifestyle. Everything anyone could want could be found in their tented cities, which were always laid out in the same way: the openings to all the tents faced south, and the royalty was in the middle, the right wing of the army on the west, and the left wing on the east. Women and children stayed in the camp, tending to the herds and keeping everything in order, while the soldiers—every able-bodied man over the age of fourteen—were out fighting battles.

1284
PIED PIPER LEGEND
130 children led out of
Hamelin, Germany

1278
REFLECTIONS
Glass mirror
invented

1276
WATER POWER
First European
paper mill

1267
STREET FIGHT
London goldsm
and tailors clas

1215
RIGHTS AND LIBERTIES
King John approves
the Magna Carta

Magna Carta

1220
GIRAFFES
First shown
in Europe

1225
COTTON
Made in
Spain

1230
DISEASE
Crusaders
bring leprosy
to Europe

1233
NEW FUEL
Coal mined
for the first
time,
Newcastle,
England

1249
AT OXFORD
First college
founded

1252
GOLD COINS
First struck
in Europe
since ancient
Rome

1266
REBIRTH BEGINS
Pre-Renaissance painter
Giotto di Bondone born

1265
DIVINE AUTHOR
Poet Dante
Alighieri born

1258
RAMPAGE
Mongols capture
Baghdad

LIFE IN A
MONGOL CITY

1 MONGOL MAPMAKERS Mongols would gather as much information as possible before moving into a new area. They often attacked their enemies from positions thought impossible.

2 MONGOL BOWMEN The Mongol army was largely a quick-moving cavalry, well armed with bows and arrows.

3 GENGHIS KHAN The most powerful man on earth in the first half of the 13th century. When he was named khan his followers told him, "We shall stand in the front of battle against your foes. When we take captive beautiful girls, we will give the best of them to you. When you hunt, we will start earliest into the field, and the beasts we bring down we will take to you. If at any time we disobey your work or do injury to you, then take from us our wives and possessions, and turn us out into the wastelands."

4 BATTLE TENT Where the regimental commanders plotted strategy.

5 NINE YAK-TAIL STANDARD A signal that Genghis Khan was present; it was displayed either in front of his tent or on the battlefield.

6 SLAVE QUARTERS The Mongols slew most of the people they conquered, but they enslaved men and women they thought would be useful to them.

7 LIVESTOCK CORRALS For generations, the nomadic Mongols had kept herds of horses, cattle, sheep, and camels.

8 TANNERY AND SADDLE MAKER

9 ARMORY Where bows, arrows, spears, and swords were repaired and made.

10 PHYSICIAN AND UNDERTAKER

11 TREASURY

12 FALCONS Excellent hunters, the Mongols enjoyed using falcons to catch their prey. Marco Polo tells of Kublai Khan (1215–94) hunting with 5,000 gyrfalcons.

13 *KESHIG* Genghis Khan's imperial guard, comprised of his most trusted men. In 1206 this elite corps was 10,000 strong, and membership was considered a supreme honor.

14 SHAMAN'S YURT The supreme Mongol deity was the Sky, and the shamans, who communicated with the gods, were the priests. When Genghis Khan rose to power, shaman Geukchu proclaimed: "The power of the Everlasting Blue Sky has descended upon him. Here on earth, he is its agent."

15 *YASA* YURT One of Genghis Khan's first deeds was to compose the *yasa*, the book of laws, which described the administration of the empire and laid out the new laws of the land.

16 GENGHIS KHAN'S YURT The ruler's tent was often made of a fine material such as linen and sometimes was even covered with gold. Staying in such tents could hardly be considered to be "roughing it." Marco Polo was received in one yurt covered in lion and leopard skins on the outside and ermine and sable on the inside; the ropes were made of silk.

17 FELT MAKING Thick pieces of felt—which was probably invented in the Mongolian region—were made from animal hair, milk, and oil.

18 DRINK The diet of the Mongols was primarily fermented mares' milk, called *ayrag*, and meat. They drank quite a lot, but drunken brawls rarely erupted: it was a crime for one Mongol to fight with another.

19 CATAPULT As the Mongols would invade a land, they would take from it what they deemed to be useful. They eagerly adopted the catapult—developed in China—and used it to great advantage.

See pages 16–17

---

1 WOMEN Women drove carts, loaded and unloaded tents, milked cows, tended the flocks, and made clothes. Occasionally they even served as reserve warriors.

2 YURT In a region where temperatures can sink to -50°F, the nomadic Mongols needed warm, portable places to live. Small yurts were easy to put up and take down, but the larger ones had to be carried on carts pulled by oxen.

3 HELMET Made of leather and brass and lined with sheepskin.

4 CHAIN-MAIL SHIRT Such lightweight armor was a prized possession, and not everyone was lucky enough to have any.

5 HORSES Like their riders, these cherished animals possessed great stamina, short legs, and immense courage.

6 QUIVERS Two quivers held short- and long-range arrows, three-foot-long armor-piercing arrows, whistling arrows, incendiary arrows, and arrows tipped with explosives.

7 CUIRASS Leather interwoven with brass protected the wearer while allowing freedom of movement.

8 BOWS Mongol bows were very stiff and very powerful. The bowstring was drawn back using a stone ring worn on the thumb.

9 *PAIZA* This identification badge was worn by messengers and guaranteed safety to the wearer throughout Mongol territory.

10 *MORIN KHOUR* This instrument had two strings and a sound box covered with animal skin. The Mongols enjoyed listening to its eerie sounds as they sat around a fire.

One of the lasting marks the Mongols and the Crusaders made on the world was that they helped open the trade routes between Asia and Europe. By the early 14th century, there was active commerce between the two continents, and the world seemed much bigger and much more interconnected.

Along with the trade goods came knowledge and information of all sorts, and by 1346 Europeans had received word of a terrible scourge in the east. Then came the awful infection itself, traveling across Asia and finally reaching the northern coast of the Black Sea, where Italian trading ships picked it up and brought it home. So began what was then called the Great Dying—the Black Plague.

By the end of 1348, the epidemic had raced through Italy, France, Spain, and Portugal and entered southern England. It then invaded Scotland, Germany, and the Baltic, and in 1351 it moved into southern Russia. In these few brutal years, the ravaging infection killed 25 million Europeans alone.

After the first wave ended, the ugly disease reared its head again and again, as it had for centuries: there were other outbreaks in 1361–62 and 1368–69 and then at least one more each decade until the end of the century, leaving behind death and destruction on an unprecedented scale.

A TRADE ROUTES
Europe was crisscrossed with land and sea trade routes.

B HOW THE PLAGUE SPREAD The plague arrived in Europe in October 1347, when sailing ships from Asia docked at Messina, Italy. The crews were dying of a mysterious disease—as were the rats on board. From there, the epidemic quickly swept northward across the continent. The Black Death was almost always fatal, killing rich and poor alike. During another plague epidemic two centuries later, English novelist Daniel Defoe wrote, "They died in heaps and were buried in heaps."

1 June 1348
2 End of 1348
3 1349
4 1351

EUROPE IN THE 14TH CENTURY: THE PLAGUE CONTINENT

1 BERGEN
2 OSLO
3 STOCKHOLM
4 COPENHAGEN
5 WARSAW
6 LUBECK

7 HAMBURG
8 BREMEN
9 AMSTERDAM
10 COLOGNE
11 FRANKFURT
12 PRAGUE
13 YORK
14 BRISTOL
15 WINCHESTER
16 LONDON
17 CHARTRES
18 PARIS
19 TROYES
20 KOBLENZ
21 STRASBOURG
22 ORLEANS
23 LA ROCHELLE
24 POITIERS
25 SANTIAGO
26 LISBON
27 TOLEDO
28 CADIZ
29 GRANADA
30 VALENCIA
31 BARCELONA
32 MARSEILLES
33 MILAN
34 VENICE
35 TRIESTE
36 GENOA
37 PISA
38 ROME
39 NAPLES
40 MESSINA
41 PALERMO

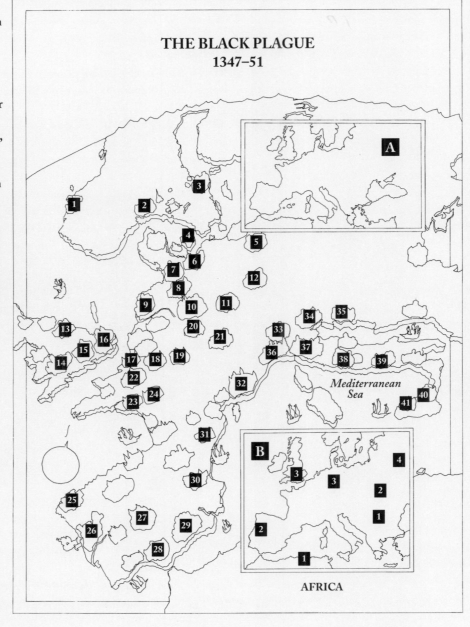

THE BLACK PLAGUE
1347–51

Mediterranean Sea

AFRICA

Epidemic: A Brutal Invasion

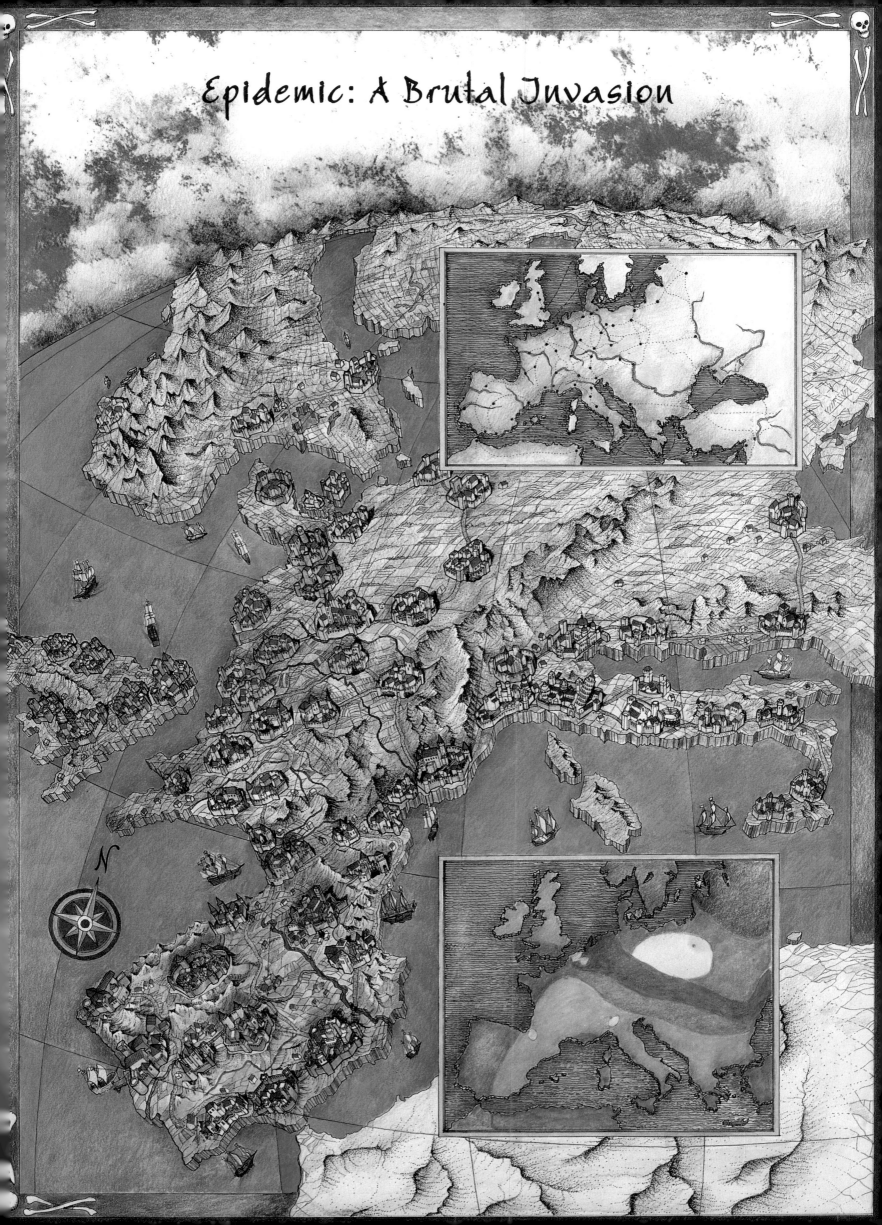

1300
APOTHE-
CARIES
Established
in Germany

1304
LOVE SONNETS
Italian scholar
Petrarch born

1398
LAST OF THE
MONGOLS
Tamerlane
sacks Delhi

1377
CARD GAMES
Displace dice,
Germany

1375
ROBIN HOOD
Appears in
English
literature

1370
HEAVY
METAL
Steel crossbow
used

Koblenz

Located at the point in western Germany where the
Rhine and Moselle rivers meet, Koblenz was a center
for river traffic. It was perfectly situated to be a thriving
trade center—and an epicenter of the plague in 1348.

Merchants, farmers, and sailors crowded into town
to do business. The city walls kept everyone in close
contact both with each other and with the filth amid
which they all lived.

Koblenz was a hothouse for the spread of disease, as
were so many other European cities at the time.

1369
BASTILLE
Built

1368
EVER GREATER
Restoration,
Great Wall
of China

1356
GERMAN MERCHANTS
UNITE
Hanseatic Trade
League formed

1351
TENNIS,
EVERYONE?
Outdoor play,
England

1305
YARD, ACRE
Edward I
standardizes
measures

1306
POGROM
France
expels Jews

1314
PRINTING
Over 60,000
characters
carved from
wooden
blocks,
China

1317
KINGS ONLY
France bars
women from
the throne

1325
AZTEC
CAPITAL
Tenochtitlán
founded

1335
THE BELL
TOLLS
Public
clock strikes
the hours,
Milan

1346
AT CALAIS
First
recorded use of
cannons in Europe

1339
DOGES'
PALACE
Venice

1337
ENGLAND VS.
FRANCE
100 Years War
begins

The Plague

1 A CITY OF BEGGARS With farms lying fallow and commerce dragging to a halt, the once-proud city of Koblenz fell into decay. Chaos reigned, and many people had to resort to asking for handouts.

2 GRIEF It is hard to imagine the agony experienced in practically every European household. One Italian man, Agnioli di Tura, wrote, "Buried with my own hands five of my children in a single grave. Many corpses were buried so superficially that the dogs dug them up and devoured them. No bells. No tears. This is the end of the world."

3 BLAME What caused the plague? The Church suggested that the victims themselves were responsible, and that the disease was God's wrath falling on them. Therefore prayer and abasement—including whipping oneself—were common. Self-flagellation caught on, and flagellants traveled from town to town in large processions, beating themselves and attempting to enlist more people into their ranks. Other people blamed the Jews (even though they too were dying of the infection), and launched vicious pogroms, second only to the Nazis' in numbers killed.

4 RODENTS The plague is spread by fleas that live on rats. Without controlling the rat population, it was not possible to control the spread of the disease—but living with rats was simply the way of life in the 14th century; they were barely even noticed unless they competed with the people for food.

5 BOARDED UP In a frenzy of despair, many city dwellers simply fled, sealing up their homes and leaving plague victims inside to rot.

6 FLEEING THE CITY Some thought that the way to stay healthy was to avoid cities, lowlands, and wet areas, and go to the mountains. In fact, moving to a lightly populated area without rodent infestation may well have saved some of those who had the means to leave.

7 IN THE WATER Some victims' bodies—human and animal—were simply thrown in the water. They eventually washed up and became food for the rats.

8 MASS BURIALS People died at such a great rate that it was impossible to provide individual graves for them all. One writer described Vienna in the summer of 1349: "There, because of the odor, and the horror inspired by the dead bodies, burials in church cemeteries were not allowed; but as soon as life was extinct the corpses were carried out of the city to a common burial place called 'God's acre.' There the deep broad pits were quickly filled to the top with the dead."

9 FIELDS LYING FALLOW When farmers died, many suffered.

See pages 22–23

---

1 THE PLAGUE There are three main types of plague. Symptoms of all include high fever, restlessness, staggering, confusion, and delirium. BUBONIC PLAGUE involves acutely inflamed and extremely painful lymph nodes under the arms and in the groin; these buboes can be as large as an egg. Most victims died within five days. The plague still occurs today in certain areas with severe rodent infestations. It can now be treated with antibiotics.

2 PNEUMONIC PLAGUE This form of plague is the only one that can be spread from person to person via a cough or sneeze. It kills 95–100% of its victims. Sneezing was a first sign of the infection, and the phrase "God bless you" came into use because the sneezer might be about to die.

3 SEPTICEMIC PLAGUE This type of the infection is the most deadly. It is always fatal. It is transmitted when a flea bites a plague victim and then transmits some infected blood while biting another person.

4 BIRD MASKS Even where and when it was available, medieval medicine—the usual remedies included purges and bleeding—was not very useful in combating the plague. In fact, the pope's own physician, Gui de Chauliac, wrote, "For self-preservation, there was nothing better than to flee the region." Physicians wore bird masks to cover their noses

in the hope of avoiding the spread of infection and also to help filter out the horrible stench of the plague. These costumes were worn as late as the 18th century when the plague would arise.

5 RELIGION Priests and nuns attempted to comfort the dying; religion relieved at least some psychic pain.

6 BLACK RATS Plague-bearing fleas rely on rats for food. When the rat dies, the flea leaves in search of another host—usually another rat—but if a rat is not available, fleas leap to another host, such as humans.

7 CHARMS AND AMULETS Many traditional remedies were tried, to no avail. People thought that garlic might help, and the best spices were said to be myrrh, saffron, and pepper. A popular magical charm used the word *abracadabra* written on a piece of paper and hung around the neck of a sick person.

RING AROUND THE ROSIE The children's game Ring around the Rosie dates to this period. "Rosie" was a rash associated with the plague; "a pocket full of posies" refers to the flowers many people carried in the belief that sweet smells were healthy (they also offset the smell of death). "Ashes, ashes, / We all fall down" is self-explanatory.

In a time when Europeans still thought the world was flat, and mariners relied on maps contrived of a dubious blend of fact, myth, and fantasy, they didn't sail very far out of the sight of land. But then in 1497, a Portuguese explorer named Vasco da Gama (1460–1524) had the courage to embark on a history-making voyage. He sailed south from Lisbon, around the Cape of Good Hope, and on to India. His goal was no religious crusade, but wealth, power, fame, new diplomatic ties—all that could be gotten from opening up a new trade route to the East.

Da Gama expected a hero's welcome in various East African trading ports along the way and in India itself, but he was in for a surprise. The busy traders he met had hardly been holding their breath, waiting for the Europeans to arrive. On the contrary, practically everyone da Gama had hoped to impress turned up their noses at his trinkets; the quality of the trade goods they saw every day overwhelmed the paltry European offerings. The traders' ships, too, were grander and more sophisticated than those built by the Portuguese.

Still, time was on the Europeans' side. Da Gama's historic accomplishment was just the first step in making the tiny country of Portugal the immensely powerful world leader it would become in the next century.

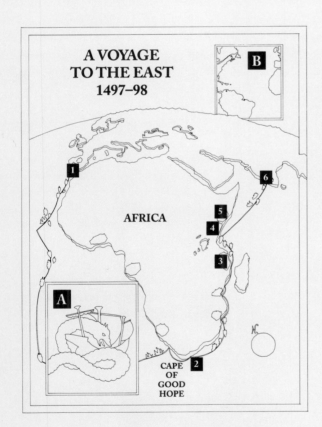

A VOYAGE TO THE EAST 1497–98

AFRICA

CAPE OF GOOD HOPE

See pages 28–29

A Sea Monster This drawing depicted what sailors in da Gama's day imagined might be waiting for them if they lost sight of land.

B Sharing the World In 1481, the pope awarded all lands south of the Canary Islands to Portugal. On May 4, 1493, he awarded all non-Christian lands west of 38° W to Spain and those to the east to Portugal. The next year, the line was moved 950 miles to the west.

1 Lisbon The capital of Portugal, located on the Tagus River.

2 Mossel Bay Ninety Africans came to stare when da Gama's ships dropped anchor here. The hungry sailors traded three bracelets for an ox.

3 Mozambique After he had sailed past endless green woodlands, this bustling city and its teeming wharves came to da Gama like a vision.

4 Mombasa Da Gama's stay here was brief. He learned that the banners hung in the city celebrated the end of Ramadan, not his arrival.

5 Malindi The sultan of this city welcomed the Portuguese sailors.

6 Calicut Da Gama's party—the first Europeans to sail to India—landed near Calicut in 1498.

A Lisbon Caravels Built along the banks of the Tagus River, these ships were in great demand all over Europe.

B Slave Trade In 1444 the Portuguese began the European slave trade. This auction is taking place in front of Lisbon's cathedral.

C Navigation Sailors use a cross-staff to determine their position.

D The Captain's Cabin Vasco da Gama plans his voyage.

E The Galley Breakfast is prepared as the rats watch.

F Raising Anchor Portuguese sailors at work.

A WORLD OF DIFFERENCE

Top to bottom: Sailors' tools included the compass, sandglass (for measuring the passage of a certain amount of time), sundial (for telling time), and cross-staff and astrolabe (for determining the angle of celestial bodies). An explorer would place a huge cross called a *padrão* in newly found land, signifying Portugal's claim to it. The *padrão* bore an inscription announcing that the king had "ordered the land to be discovered."

1400
TO TOWNS
Anasazi people abandon cliff dwellings

1403
FLORENCE BAPTISTRY
Lorenzo Ghiberti works on doors

1404
TRADING PARTNERS
Japan and China

Below: Spices were used to mask the taste of rotten food. Clockwise from left: cloves, pepper, cinnamon bark, nutmeg.

LISBON HARBOR

The city of Lisbon overlooked its bustling waterfront. Many men and women who lived by and for the sea —explorers, mapmakers, shipbuilders, navigators, and fishermen—crowded into the city from all over Europe.

The waters teemed with boats of all sorts, but the finest was the caravel, which had both square and triangular lateen sails, allowing sailors for the first time to sail well both with and against the wind.

With this innovation, mariners could go anywhere they wanted and know they'd be able to get back. The horizons beckoned.

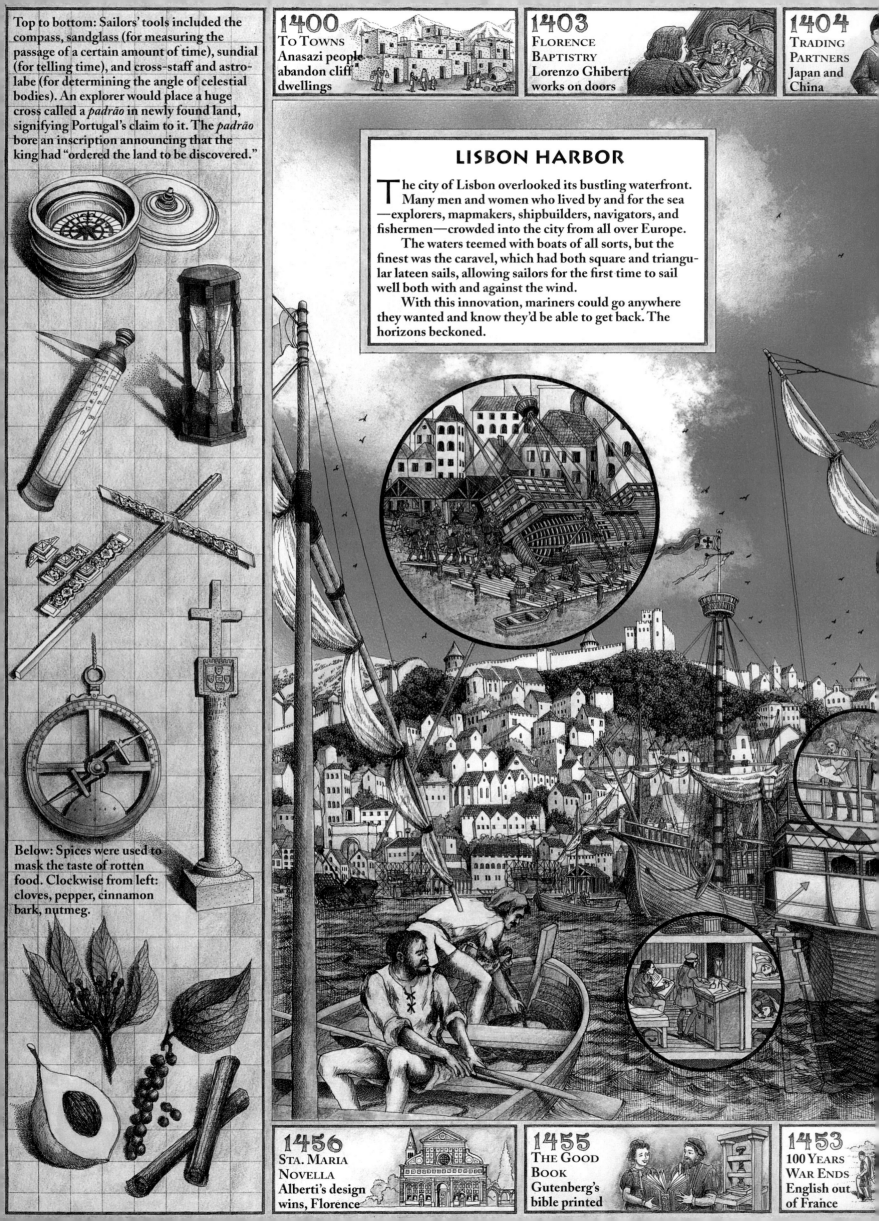

1456
STA. MARIA NOVELLA
Alberti's design wins, Florence

1455
THE GOOD BOOK
Gutenberg's bible printed

1453
100 YEARS WAR ENDS
English out of France

1419
MADEIRA ISLANDS
Portuguese
plant sugarcane

1422
CHINESE
TO AFRICA
Trade for
exotic animals

1431
MARTYR
Joan of Arc
burned at the
stake

1432
DAVID BY
DONATELLO
Completed

1433
TIMBUKTU
Taken by
Tuareg
nomads

1450
POWER
Great
Zimbabwe
at its zenith

1441
FLEMISH
MASTER
Jan van Eyck
dies

1434
ARTS PATRON
Cosimo de' Medici
seizes power in
Florence

Mozambique, the southern edge of Muslim civilization, was one of a string of independent city-states on the East African coast. The day-to-day governing was overseen by a sultan who lived within the walls of the *kasbah*, or citadel, along with various ministers, dignitaries, scholars, professors, and wealthy merchants. The rest of the population resided in densely populated neighborhoods surrounding the *kasbah*.

Life in Mozambique was peaceful—though the city-states did not get along, they were too busy with other matters to wage war. Instead, the focus was business. The people spoke Swahili at home and Arabic in the marketplace and traded gold, ivory, iron, timber, and tortoiseshell for silk, pearls, porcelain, rubies, spices, and dates. They dressed in fine linen robes and wrapped their heads in silk embroidered with gold thread. Their port was filled with all manner of ships from the east—huge Chinese ocean going junks, Arab dhows, and boats from Malaysia, Molucca, and southeast Asia. The city bustled with traffic.

The Portuguese had planned their expedition very carefully, but da Gama and his men were flabbergasted to find that Mozambique was no primitive village. No one had dreamed they'd encounter such riches and sophistication in a remote East African port. Da Gama's ships—the caravels that were so prized in Europe—were dwarfed here. And the goods they had carried thousands of miles around the continent—caps, glass beads, copper bowls, little round bells, tin rings, and bracelets to give to rulers and striped cotton cloth, olive oil, sugar, and coral to trade for spices—seemed almost worthless.

The situation was made very clear to the Portuguese explorer when he invited the sultan of Mozambique on board his ship and tried to ply him with the sort of gifts that had impressed some African tribal leaders he'd met earlier on his journey. To da Gama's surprise and dismay, the sultan was not at all interested, and was in fact insulting. "He treated all we gave him with contempt and asked for scarlet cloth, of which we had none," a chronicler reported. Meanwhile, the sailors had been trying to trade with the people they met, and had been barely able to exchange some glass beads for some goats and pigeons—nothing more.

Da Gama soon moved on, his focus on India.

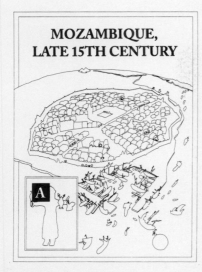

See pages 32–33

A FOREIGNER This figure of a Portuguese soldier was carved by an East African. The Portuguese, from an entirely different world, were both more ruthless and better armed than the Africans.

A SCORN Da Gama meets an African ruler who disdains the Portuguese trade goods—they're not up to his usual standards.

B EXOTIC BEASTS Animals from the interior of Africa are brought to Mozambique to be sold and shipped to Asia and Europe.

AN AFRICAN TRADING CITY

1457
FUTEBALL, GOLFE
Parliament bans new games. Scotland's army needs archers

1458
IN ATHENS
Turks sack Acropolis

1462
SONGHAI EMPIRE
Rules in eastern Mali

1465
PLATFORM SHOES
Chopines are the rage in Euro[pe]

1498
TOOTHBRUSH INVENTED
The Chinese dramatically improve dental hygiene

1497
THE LAST SUPPER
Leonardo da Vinci finishes masterpiece

1494
TWO WORLD POWERS
Spain and Portugal split the world

1493
THANKS, COLUMBUS
Pineapples in Europe

THE MARKET

Mozambique's market was noisy and active. Almost everything imaginable was traded there, including silk, porcelain, ivory, spices, animals, and slaves. The air was filled with a hubbub of languages spoken by people from at least a dozen nations.

Far right, top to bottom: The greater a Rendille woman's status, the larger her woven palm-fiber collar; this Fulani girl's coins and amber beads identify her as an unmarried nomad; a young Ait Hadiddou woman of Morocco wears

(continued on opposite page)

1492
GOODBYE, COLUMBUS
Sets out on first voyage

1489
SHORTHAND
Symbols for plus and minus used for the first time

1487
20,000 AZTEC SACRIFICES
Tenochtitlán temple dedicated

1483
SILVER PAVILION
Yoshimasa's Kyoto retreat

1466
HUMANIST AND
REFORMER
Erasmus
born

1469
TOGETHER
Ferdinand and
Isabella marry,
unifying Spain

(continued from opposite page)
this costume to a festival where men seek
wives; only a Zulu nobleman is allowed to
wear leopard skin; this Samburu coiffure is
made from sisal, cloth, ocher, and fat; cast
bronze bracelet, West Africa; Swahili silver anklet; gold earrings, Mali; ivory
spoon with a
Portuguese
soldier; and
ivory bracelets
studded with
hundreds of
lead beads

1478
SPANISH
INQUISITION
Brutal cam-
paign begun

1477
IN BOLOGNA
Movable-type
printing press
prints music

❁ *Florence, 16th century* ❁

Florence has often been called the "cradle of the Renaissance," for it was here that a unique mixture of philoso-phers, painters, sculptors, scholars, and merchants thrived in an environment perfectly suited to them all. The city was simultaneously an intellectual and artistic center and a business capital. This may seem like a contradiction, but the fact is that the wealthy merchants and powerful businessmen there made the rich cultural life possible.

This freewheeling, flamboyant era was populated by towering personalities, the grandest of whom belonged to the Medici family. The family had a tremendously successful banking business with branches in sixteen European capitals. As their riches produced more riches, the Medicis commissioned countless works of art and topped the bids of rival states for the services of the greatest painters, sculptors, and teachers. In the spirit of the era, the most famous and powerful Medici, Lorenzo (1449–92), was simply called "the Magnificent." A skilled poet himself, he filled his home with philosophers and artists and at one point spent more than half the state's annual income on books.

In the Renaissance—literally "rebirth"—an effort was made to emulate the glorious days of classical civilization in scholarship and art. Florence, "the new Athens on the Arno," was at the center of it all.

A *THE CANON OF PROPORTIONS* Created by Leonardo da Vinci, this is one of the most famous drawings ever made, neatly combining the artist's twin interests of art and science.

B PALAZZO VECCHIO Florence's crenellated town hall, capped by its distinctive bell tower, is where the governing body, the Signoria, sat. Members of the Signoria served for only two months, so there was constant jostling for power. Lions, the symbol of Florentine freedom, lived in a pit nearby.

1 STA. MARIA DI CARIGNANO, GENOA

2 STA. MARIA DELLE GRAZIE, MILAN Donato Bramante built the east end of this monumental cathedral at the same time that Leonardo da Vinci was painting the *Last Supper* in the refectory.

3 ASINELLI AND GARISENDA TOWERS, BOLOGNA In the Renaissance, there were hundreds of towers in Florence and Bologna. These two, built in the 12th century, are still major landmarks.

4 STA. MARIA DEI MIRACOLI, VENICE The facade of this church (1481–89) is decorated with colored marble panels.

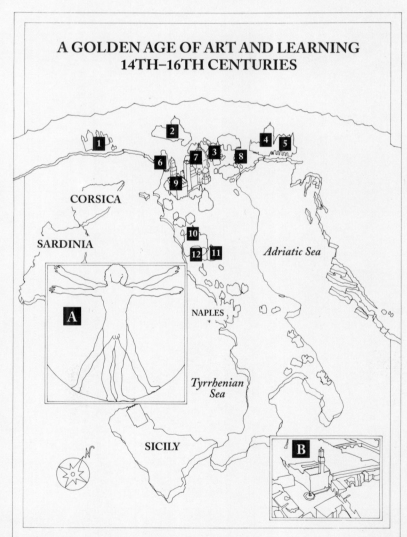

A GOLDEN AGE OF ART AND LEARNING
14TH–16TH CENTURIES

CORSICA

SARDINIA

Adriatic Sea

NAPLES

Tyrrhenian Sea

SICILY

5 S. GIORGIO MAGGIORE, VENICE Designed by Andrea Palladio in 1565, this magnificent structure demonstrates the striving for classical qualities that was popular at the time.

6 TOWER OF PISA This is the bell tower for Pisa Cathedral, part of a group of magnificent Romanesque buildings that also includes the Baptistry to the west.

7 STA. MARIA DEL FIORE, FLORENCE A dome by Filippo Brunelleschi crowns this famous cathedral.

8 S. APOLLINARE, RAVENNA

9 PALAZZO VECCHIO, FLORENCE

10 ST. PETER'S, ROME This cathedral is widely considered to be the most ambitious structure of the 16th century.

11 TEMPIETTO, ROME Designed in the early 16th century by Bramante, this chapel (called "little temple") marks the site of St. Peter's crucifixion.

12 COLOSSEUM, ROME An enormous amphitheater built in the years 72–80 as a site for gladiatorial games.

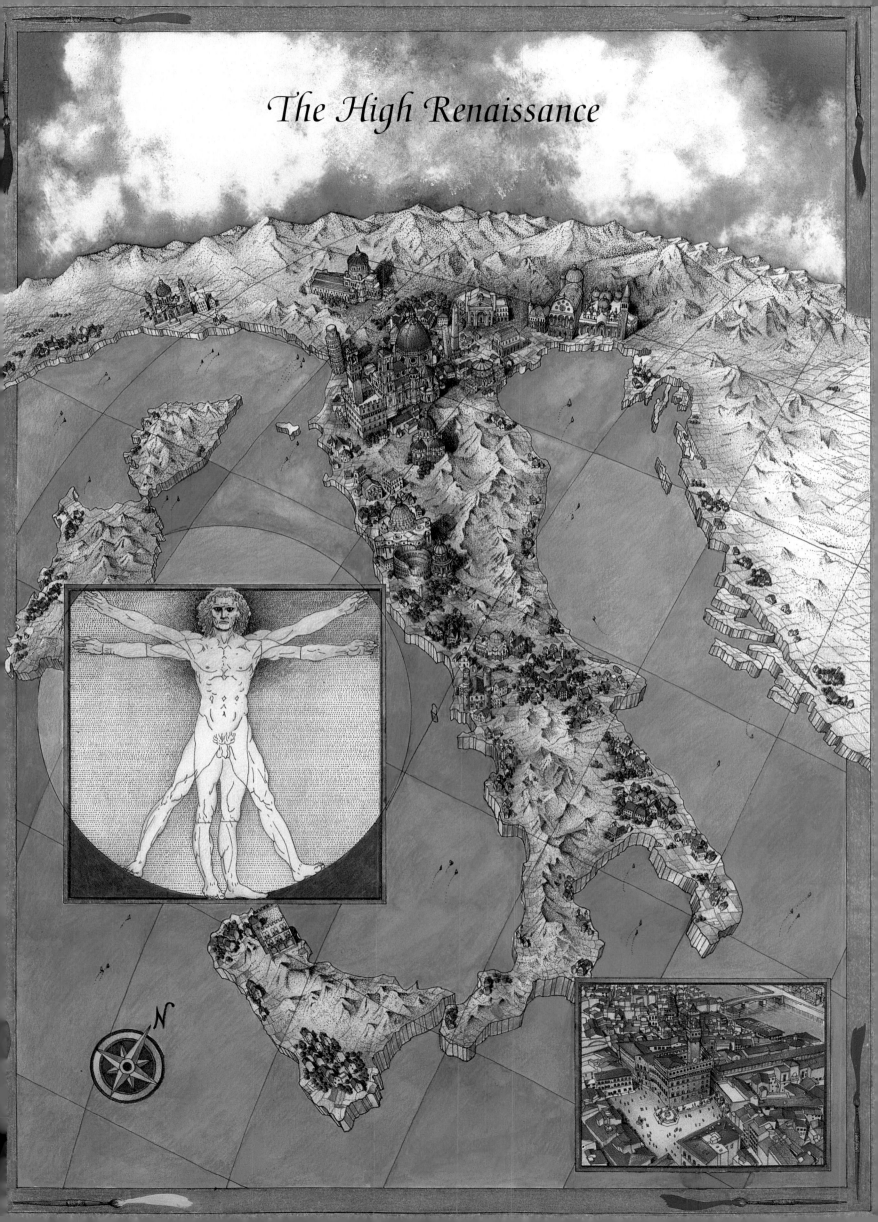

The High Renaissance

1502
CLASSICAL DOME
Donato Bramante
completes his
Tempietto, Rome

1506
ANCIENT
MASTERPIECE
Laocoön is
uncovered

1510
FROM THE
AMERICAS
Sunflowers intro-
duced in Europe

1512
COPERNICUS
Writes that the
earth revolves
around the sun

The New Athens

Printers, booksellers, clothmakers, goldsmiths, wax-figure makers, bankers, and artists mingled on Florence's busy streets. It is almost beyond belief that some of the most famous artists and architects of all time—Leonardo da Vinci, Michelangelo Buonarroti, Sandro Botticelli, Titian, Raphael, and plenty of others—lived and worked in Florence in the 16th century.

How extraordinary that these men knew each other and each other's work, had studios close by, and ate and talked together in this golden city.

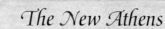

1599
PLAYHOUSE
Globe Theater
built, London

1596
VOLCANIC ERUPTION
Mount Hekla,
Iceland

1573
BOY EMPEROR
China's Wan Li
assumes throne at
the age of ten

1569
A NEW
PROJECTION
Mercator pub-
lishes map

1565
ST. AUGUSTIN
Europeans sett
permanently in
North America

1517
FROM ARABIA
Coffee comes
to Europe

1519
IMPORT
Cortés brings
horses to the
New World

1520
SULTAN OF
TURKEY
Selim I dies

1533
PIZARRO
TRIUMPHS
Inca king
Atahualpa
executed

1535
EXECUTED
Sir Thomas
More

1560
FEUDAL BARON
Oda Nobunaga routs
Imagawa clan, unify-
ing Japan

1558
CROWNED
Elizabeth I rises to
the English throne

1555
IVAN THE TERRIBLE
Starts construction
of St. Basil's
Cathedral

Two
Masters

1 LEONARDO DA VINCI'S STUDIO Leonardo once described the conditions that would be ideal for a painter: "His house is clean and filled with charming pictures; and often he is accompanied by music or by the reading of various and beautiful works." Here he works in just such a place, surrounded by his notebooks and painting paraphernalia. The *Mona Lisa*, which he kept until he died, hangs on the wall.

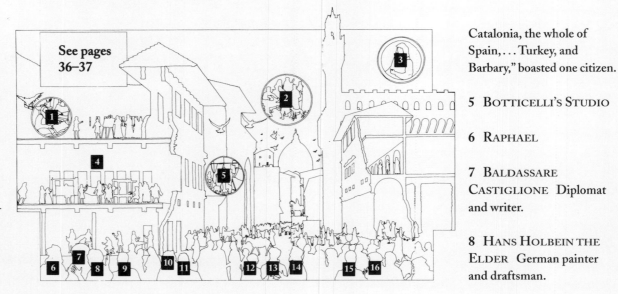

See pages 36–37

Catalonia, the whole of Spain,...Turkey, and Barbary," boasted one citizen.

5 BOTTICELLI'S STUDIO

6 RAPHAEL

7 BALDASSARE CASTIGLIONE Diplomat and writer.

8 HANS HOLBEIN THE ELDER German painter and draftsman.

2 BANKERS The seventy-two bankers of Florence did their work on tables set up outside. They lent money and changed it as well—a necessary service, as each of the almost two dozen Italian states had its own system of currency. The Medici bank also sold traveler's checks, which had been devised in the Middle Ages as a safe way of carrying money.

3 LORENZO DE' MEDICI The patronage and leadership of the Medici family helped make Florence what it was in the Renaissance. Though they were all magnificent leaders and benefactors in their own ways, Lorenzo's ebullience, charm, sense of humor, and stylishness made him especially beloved.

4 MAKING WOOLEN CLOTH At this time almost everyone wore wool, much of it from Florence. Florentine merchants imported fleece from as far as England and Portugal, and then it was beaten, picked, washed, combed, carded, spun, woven, and dyed in the lustrous scarlets, browns, and blues the city was known for. In the 15th century Florence had 270 wool shops and 83 silk warehouses, which furnished "gold and silver stuffs, velvet, brocade, damask, taffeta, and satin to Rome, Naples,

9 TITIAN

10 ALBRECHT DÜRER The German master made two extended trips to Italy, where he breathed the air of the Renaissance.

11 NICCOLÒ MACHIAVELLI The Italian political philosopher and secretary to the Florentine executive council wrote *The Prince* in 1513.

12 LUCREZIA BORGIA Her court at Ferrara was a gathering place for scholars, poets, and artists.

13 CARDINAL PIETRO BEMBO Titian painted his portrait.

14 CESARE BORGIA Known for his ruthless military conquests.

15 LEONARDO LOREDAN The doge, or ruler, of Venice from 1501 to 1521. His palace was decorated by Titian, Tintoretto, and Veronese.

16 Patrons of the arts mingled with all the great names of the day.

Although neither Leonardo nor Michelangelo was born in Florence, both grew up professionally there, under the sponsorship of Lorenzo de' Medici. The two masters are said to have disliked each other—they certainly had a rivalry—but they did share a love for the city of Florence.

1 MICHELANGELO (1475–1564) Lorenzo noticed the young artist when he was a student at art school and took him into his palace, treating him as one of the family.

2 SKETCH FOR THE *LIBYAN SIBYL* For his first drawing of the figure of this great seer from Greek myth, Michelangelo used a male model.

3 FACE OF *DAVID* Michelangelo carved his nude, fourteen-foot-tall *David* when he was only twenty-nine years old. One city official complained that David's nose was too big, so Michelangelo hid a handful of marble dust in his palm and spilled it as he tapped the nose with a chisel. The official pronounced that he was pleased with the (unchanged) result.

4 *LIBYAN SIBYL* The masculine lines in the drawing were softened for the fresco, which is in the Sistine Chapel in Rome.

5 LEONARDO (1452–1519) After many years in Milan, Leonardo came back to Florence in early 1503, in search of creative stimulation. The advice he always gave painters—and followed himself—was to "look carefully" and study nature.

6 SKETCH FOR *THE LAST SUPPER* In 1495 Leonardo started painting *The Last Supper*, which would take him more than two years to complete. He used an experimental combination of oil, varnish, and pigments, which proved to be a failure—the painting was reported to be disintegrating as early as 1517. Its subject is Christ predicting that "one of you shall betray me."

7 GROTESQUES People said Leonardo had no sense of humor, but his notebooks were filled with these wild caricatures.

8 *ANGEL'S HEAD* This polished 1483 sketch is for one of the figures in Leonardo's masterpiece *The Virgin of the Rocks*.

9 MOTOR Leonardo was fascinated by how things work from an early age. While serving as apprentice to the painter Andrea del Verrocchio he was already sketching devices of all sorts. He left thousands of pages of notes and sketches when he died; some 5,700 survive today.

☸ OSAKA, 17th Century ☸

For Japan, the 16th century was one of endless unrest, as fierce daimyos—feudal lords with vast holdings defended by samurai armies—warred among themselves, building great castles to protect their domains. Out of this chaos, three great leaders—Oda Nobunaga (1534–1582), Toyotomi Hideyoshi (1536–1598), and Tokugawa Ieyasu (1543–1616)—arose who shaped their nation's destiny.

A minor daimyo, Nobunaga was a military genius who united many powerful feudal houses in the 1560s and took over the imperial capital of Kyōto in 1568. His general Hideyoshi, a prodigious castlebuilder, took the reins of power when Nobunaga was betrayed by one of his lieutenants in 1582 and proved to be a superb administrator, ruling central Japan. The daimyo Ieyasu quickly emerged as the victor in the power struggle that followed Hideyoshi's death in 1598, but it took him years to destroy the power of the Toyotomi: his army finally overthrew their last stronghold, Osaka Castle, in 1615, completing Japan's unification. Thus, the 17th century saw the beginning of a peaceful and properous period in Japanese history that lasted two centuries.

In 1614, Ieyasu made a momentous decision that had an enormous influence on Japan's future: he required all Japanese Christians to join Buddhist temples and banished foreign priests, out of the fear that the Christians would undermine his political authority among his restless retinue of daimyos. His successors soon passed laws that cut off Japan from almost all contact with Westerners, and the country remained officially closed to foreigners until 1854.

1 OSAKA CASTLE The castles of the daimyos consisted of tall wooden keeps armored with plaster or clay, raised up on high stone bases. Hideyoshi took three years (1583–86) and many thousands of workers to build Osaka Castle, the largest in Japan. The Tokugawa rebuilt the castle after conquering it, but the keep finally burned in 1868.

2 MARUOKA CASTLE Built in 1576, this is called the floating castle, on account of its wide moat.

3 MATSUMOTO CASTLE Begun in 1504 and completed by Hideyoshi in 1597, this castle is notable for its striking white plaster walls and black woodwork.

4 HIMEJI CASTLE Formerly Hideyoshi's, this strategically vital castle was taken over by the Tokugawa in 1601 and expanded into one of the most spectacular in Japan.

5 KINKAKUJI, KYŌTO Kyōto had been the old imperial capital of Japan since 749, but by the 16th century, it was in deep decline. Hideyoshi reconstructed the city, but after Ieyasu established his base in eastern Japan, Kyōto, with its many temples and shrines, became solely a cultural center. Among its treasures is the late 14th century Kinkakuji, or Gold Pavilion, the former pleasure villa of a shogun transformed into a temple after his death.

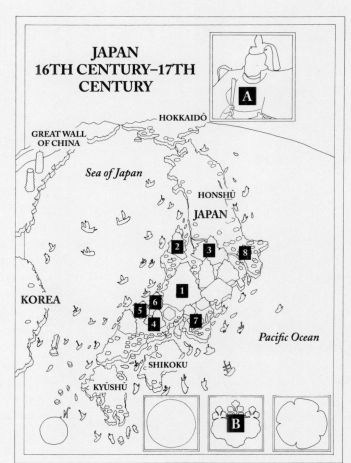

6 GINKAKUJI, KYŌTO The tea ceremony originated at the Ginkakuji, or Silver Pavilion, another villa turned temple, built in 1483.

7 TŌDAIJI, NARA Completed in 752, this monastery houses an enormous bronze statue of the Buddha in the largest wooden building in the world.

8 EDO Ieyasu led his retainers into the swamps of Edo in 1590. There he built his castle. It took more than a century for the village to surpass Osaka and Kyōto in size, but over time it became Japan's largest city: Tokyo.

A In 1603 the emperor made Ieyasu shogun ("barbarian-subduing generalissimo")—the nation's chief military, political, and economic figure—marking the beginning of the Tokugawa Shogunate, which ruled until 1867.

B Family crests of the "Three Heroes" of Japanese unification: right, Oda Nobunaga, the first to use European firearms in battle, who once told a missionary, "Do not worry about either the emperor or the shogun. I am in complete control of everything;" center, Toyotomi Hideyoshi, himself a commoner, who instituted laws to enforce social stability and disarmed all but the warrior classes; left, Tokugawa Ieyasu, who carefully consolidated the power of the Tokugawa.

A LAND OF CASTLES

1662
NEW REIGN
IN CHINA
Emperor
K'ang-hsi

1666
VIOLIN MAKER
Antonio
Stradivari in
business

1668
FIRST
REFLECTOR
Isaac Newton's
telescope

1681
EXTINCTION OF A
SPECIES
Last Dodo dies

1689
OUT OF AFRICA
Arabs eject
Portuguese

1600
TOKUGAWA
VICTORY
Ieyasu wins
Battle of
Sekigahara

A Great Castle Falls

Osaka had been a trading center since the 4th century, thanks to its harbor and navigable rivers, and
it grew enormously after Hideyoshi built his stronghold.
Ieyasu spent the better part of a year conquering the
castle, and he succeeded only because some moats had
been filled in and walls razed during a temporary peace.
When the fortress fell, the town's merchants quickly
declared their allegiance to Ieyasu and the city continued
to prosper as a commercial center. By mid-century, the
Tokugawa Shogunate carefully supervised the construction of new castles, ending an era.

1605
SPANISH
NOVEL
Don Quixote

1608
FRENCH
SETTLEMENT
Champlain at
Quebec

1620
PLYMOUTH TO
PLYMOUTH
Pilgrims in
Massachusetts

1632
AT AGRA
Work begins
on Taj Mahal

1637
PHILOSOPHICAL
PROGRESS
René Descartes's
masterwork

1642
EUROPEAN
EXPEDITION
To Tasmania
and New
Zealand

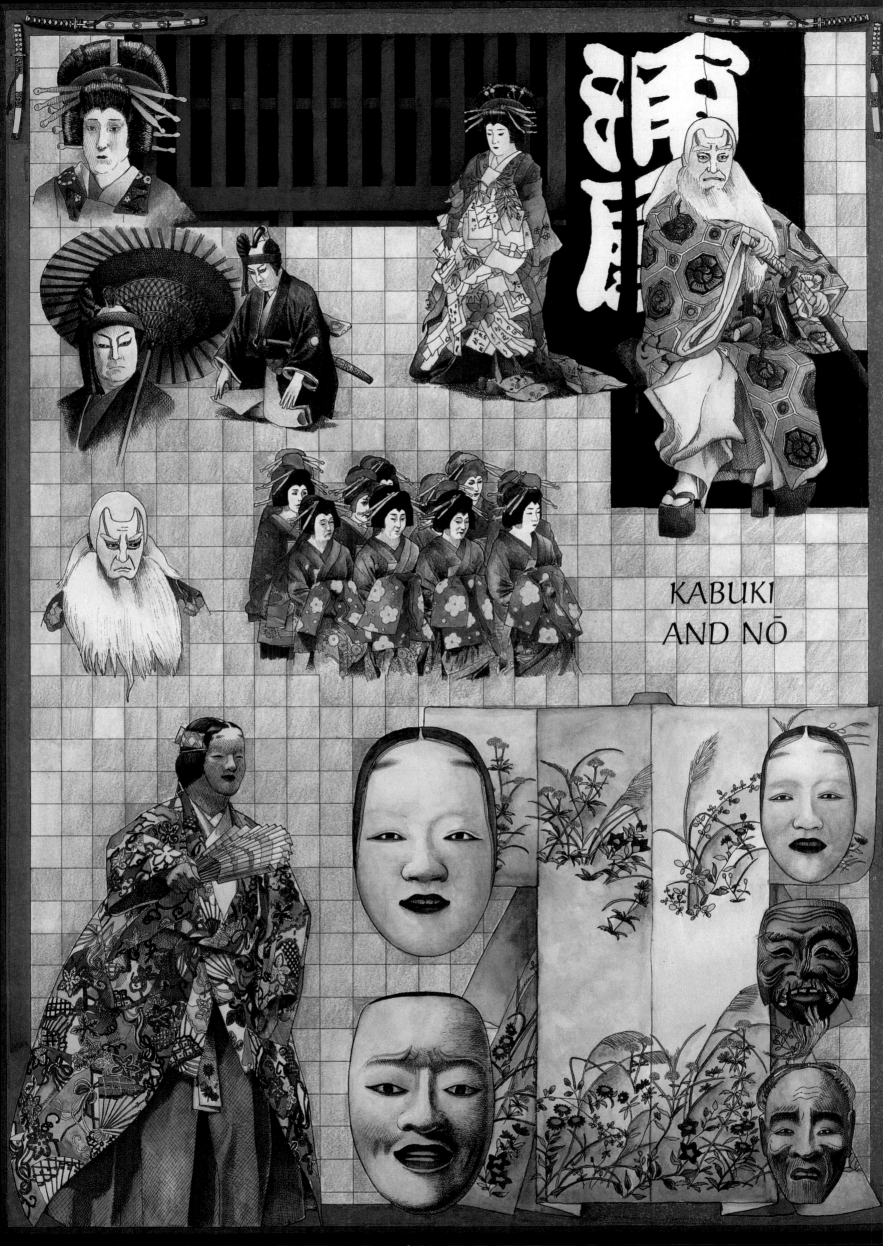

KABUKI
AND NŌ

1 Ieyasu sent an army of 180,000 to take Osaka castle, which was surrounded by a network of rivers, canals, moats, and walls measuring nine miles around. Ninety thousand men, led by Hideyoshi's son Hideyori, successfully defended the fortress for months. The attacking samurai, advancing behind heavy wooden shields (a tactic of Nobunaga's), had to traverse narrow bridges under a hail of fire to reach the keep.

2 Heavy iron gates were set so that attackers would have to make a 90° turn in order to approach them, creating bottlenecks.

3 The samurai kept their weapons in the castle armory. It is certainly possible that Portuguese missionaries told the Japanese about their castles back home, which may explain this room's similarity to a European castle keep. Originally military retainers of local lords, samurai (the word means "one who serves") developed into the feudal warrior class that ruled Japan from the late 12th century until 1868. Samurai clothing was strictly regulated, with members of each rank wearing specific garments; breaking

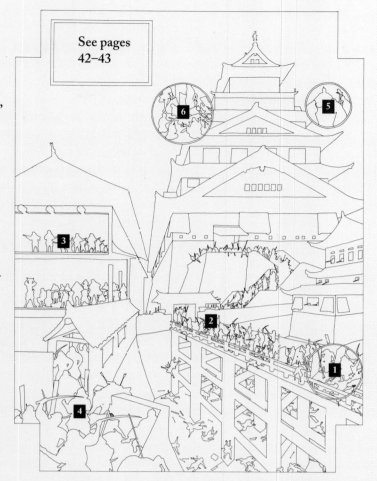

See pages 42–43

these and other strict rules of conduct resulted in punishment. A samurai would not be seen without his pair of swords—the samurai symbol—and a folding fan stuck into the sash of his robe.

4 The castle had many traps. For example, paths were cleverly sited so that they funneled attacking samurai into small areas were defenders could surprise them.

5 Since Ieyasu had outlawed Christianity, many Christian samurai took refuge with the Toyotomi forces in Osaka castle. A Jesuit inside the castle reported, "There were so many crosses, Jesu's and Sant'Iago's on their flags, tents, and other martial insignia which the Japanese use in their encampments, that this must needs have made Ieyasu sick to his stomach."

6 The daimyo and his entourage only occupied the castle keep in times of war. After a cannon blast killed two servants in the castle's emergency siege quarters, Hideyoshi's widow convinced her son to surrender to Ieyasu.

KABUKI Kabuki, Japan's tremendously popular theater tradition, began around the turn of the 17th century, when a young woman named Okuni organized a troupe of dancers to perform outdoors in Kyōto. Their performances, combining elements of the Nō drama and the latest songs and dances, attracted large crowds. The unconventional kabuki theater unsettled the Tokugawa Shogunate, and laws were passed between 1629 and 1657 limiting the right to perform to adult men and establishing theater districts where the actors could live and work. These laws led to the rise of the onnagata, a kabuki actor who specializes in female roles.

Sukeroku is one of the most famous Kabuki plays, in which a young commoner, Sukeroku, and a samurai named Ikyu fight over Agemaki, a courtesan.

1 SUKEROKU The dashing young man enters, jauntily twirling an umbrella.

2 AGEMAKI The courtesan and Sukeroku exchange vows of love.

3 IKYU Infuriated by Sukeroku and envious of the attention the young man receives from the courtesans, the samurai reaches for his sword.

4 COURTESANS Courtesans are grouped so that they focus the audience's attention toward the center of interest

NŌ The Nō drama seems to have been the creation of a Buddhist priest in the late 14th century. It evolved into a theatrical tradition for men, retaining many religious elements. Many of the great samurai, including Hideyoshi, were able performers; in fact, it was expected that a ranking samurai would be able to chant certain Nō verses.

5 *EGUCHI* The character Kan'ami, from the Nō drama *Eguchi*, which takes place during the Tokugawa Shogunate. The actor wears a zō mask and a karaori costume, one of the most elaborate in the Nō theater.

6 ZŌ The mask of a classically beautiful young woman. The teeth are stained black and the eyebrows are plucked and then redrawn high up on the forehead.

7 KANTAN-OTOKO The main character in the play *Kantan* wears this mask.

8 FUKAI The mask of a middle-aged woman.

9 KOKUSHIKI This mask is used in a dance celebrating abundant harvests.

10 KOJŌ The old man depicted by this mask is noble and godlike.

♪ Vienna, 18th century ♪

For centuries Vienna has been a great center of power and wealth. In 1282 the city became the official seat of the Habsburg dynasty, under whose control it would remain for almost 650 years. Vienna became the capital of the vast Holy Roman Empire in 1558, and (with only one exception) the Habsburgs, now even more powerful, presided over the city until 1918.

Of course, all great powers have enemies, and one of the Habsburgs' was the Turks, who besieged Vienna in 1683. When they were finally driven off, the Turks left behind a huge supply of coffee beans, the value of which was not immediately clear to the Viennese—they did not yet drink coffee. One far-seeing man took the beans and established the city's first coffeehouse. Today, the Viennese coffeehouse is as fabled as the Parisian café and the London pub—a local gathering place where a sense of camaraderie is as important as the drink itself.

The Habsburgs brought riches and stability to the city, and, especially in the 17th and 18th centuries, a spirit of open-mindedness prevailed. Vienna was the crossroads of the Germanic, Slav, Italian, and Hungarian cultures, and the influence of its foreign visitors is reflected in its architecture and music. The impact of Italian architects and artists, who were retreating from the classical Renaissance style, is especially clear in many buildings constructed during this time. Capturing Vienna's liveliness, these new buildings were designed in the highly decorated style called Baroque.

The same creative ferment led to a love affair between Vienna and Italian composers and performers. Local heroes Franz Joseph Haydn, Wolfgang Amadeus Mozart, and Ludwig van Beethoven (who moved there from Germany at the age of twenty-two) were also a source of great pride. Today, music still pervades Vienna—in the grand concert halls and in the streets, where strolling musicians may echo the thoughts of many as they sing this song: "Vienna, Vienna, you alone shall always be the city of my dreams."

A LOCATION, LOCATION, LOCATION Vienna is situated in the center of Europe, its hills sloping down to the Danube River. St. Michael's Square (Michaelerplatz) marks the intersection of Kohlmarkt and Herrengasse, two of Vienna's most elegant streets. Several Mozart operas were performed first in the nearby Burgtheater, including *The Abduction from the Seraglio, Così Fan Tutte,* and *The Marriage of Figaro.*

1 ST. PETER'S CHURCH (PETERSKIRCHE) This Baroque building (built 1702–33) stands on the site of Vienna's first church, built in the 4th century.

2 ST. STEPHEN'S CATHEDRAL (STEPHANSDOM) A symbol of Vienna, this Gothic cathedral has been damaged by warfare three times, most severely in World War II. A plan to add a second tower in the 16th century was abandoned in favor of strengthening the city's fortifications against the Turks.

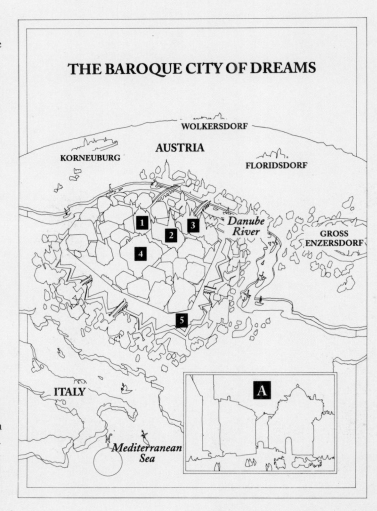

THE BAROQUE CITY OF DREAMS

WOLKERSDORF

AUSTRIA

KORNEUBURG

FLORIDSDORF

Danube River

GROSS ENZERSDORF

ITALY

Mediterranean Sea

3 JESUIT CHURCH (JESUITEN-KIRCHE) The swirling Baroque decorations on the interior of this church, built in 1623–27, have been dubbed "Jesuit snails." Emperor Ferdinand, a Catholic, summoned the Jesuits to Vienna in the mid-16th century to end the Protestant Reformation in the then predominantly Protestant city. They were successful; today 95 percent of Viennese are Catholic.

4 HOFBURG The Imperial Palace of the Habsburgs was constantly rebuilt between the 13th and 19th centuries, resulting in the mostly Baroque ensemble as it exists today.

5 FORTIFICATIONS Vienna's fortifications protected the city from the Turks in the 16th and 17th centuries, but by the 19th century, warfare had changed and they were obsolete —Napoleon entered the city twice without firing a shot. By 1865 they had been replaced with an elegant promenade called the Ring.

1701
AN EMPIRE IS BORN
Ashanti defeat Denkyira

1703
NAMESAKE
Peter the Great founds St. Petersburg

1707
ERUPTION
Mt. Fuji, Japan

1710
ST. PAUL'S CATHEDRAL
Completed in London

1792
GUILLOTINE
Now symbol of the French Revolution

1782
HOT AIR
Humans fly in new balloons

1781
HEAVENLY DISCOVERY
Herschel finds Uranus

1776
A NEW NATION
Signing of Declaration of Independence

1773
FIRST CAST-IRON SPAN
Bridge built, England

1768
CAPTAIN JAMES COOK
Sails to Pacific for the first time

1714
WEATHER
REPORT
Fahrenheit scale
developed

1723
MICROSCOPIST
DIES
Antoni van
Leeuwenhoek

1727
COFFEE
First planted
in Brazil

1736
CH'ING
DYNASTY
Chi-en Lung
becomes
emperor

1747
HOW SWEET
IT IS
Sugar
found in
beets

A Glittering Evening

On the evening of September 30, 1791, Vienna's
Theater auf der Wieden was packed with dignitaries.
This was to be a triumphant premiere, one of unequaled
proportions—Mozart's last opera, *The Magic Flute*,
would be performed for the first time. All Vienna knew of
Mozart's poor health (he would die two months later at
the age of thirty-five).

The concert hall, since destroyed, was a Baroque
monument. Statuary, soaring columns, paintings, chan-
deliers, and other decorations—along with thousands of
candles—all helped make the evening sparkle.

1759
BEST-SELLER
Voltaire
publishes
Candide

1753
PLANTS
CLASSIFIED
By Carolus
Linnaeus

1752
ELECTRICITY
Ben Franklin's
lightning
rod

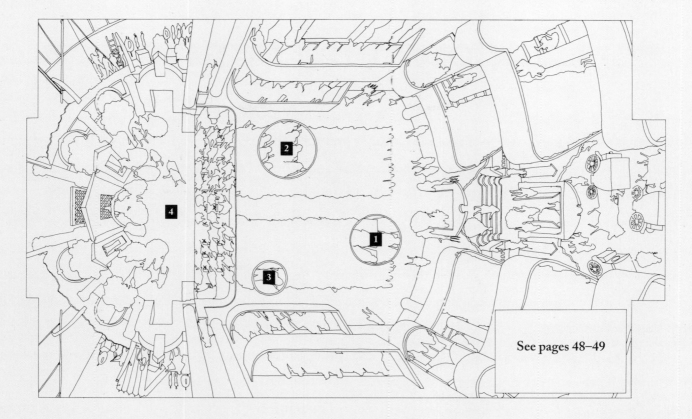

See pages 48–49

Although there are no firsthand accounts of who was present at the premiere of *The Magic Flute*, for this illustration I have used my imagination and assembled some of the first citizens of Europe who might have wished to come from near and far to be present at the much heralded event.

1 JANE AUSTEN AND NAPOLEON Since Mozart was the most celebrated composer in Europe, it is likely that the concert hall was packed with notables of every stripe. Austen, we know, never left England, but it was irresistible to imagine the sixteen-year-old who would become the finest novelist of her day at the triumph of the greatest composer. A genius of a different sort, Napoleon, at the time an aspiring officer of twenty-two with a taste for Mozart's music, might also have liked to be there. Just a few decades later, he "returned" to Austria, this time with his invading troops.

2 BEETHOVEN AND HAYDN The fifty-nine-year-old Franz Joseph Haydn, who was Mozart's teacher and a close friend, was almost certainly at the premiere. He was one of the most prolific of all composers; he wrote 106 symphonies, 83 string quartets, 54 piano sonatas, 23 operas, and many other pieces. The twenty-one-year-old Beethoven had met Mozart in 1787 when he first visited Vienna. He moved there a year after the concert pictured here, in 1792, to study with Haydn: wouldn't he have loved to be able to hear this!

3 SALIERI Also in attendance I have included the forty-one-year-old Antonio Salieri, the hugely popular composer whom Mozart distrusted to the point of thinking him a poisoner.

4 *THE MAGIC FLUTE* A contemporary writer said, "Never has a dramatic work caused more general felicity for any nation."

---

1 DRAWING ROOM In the 18th century, music was enjoyed in private—in salons—much more often than in public. People would come together in small groups to sing at the piano or play sonatas or chamber music. Haydn, Mozart, and Beethoven all composed a substantial amount of chamber music, especially string quartets.

2 MOZART'S FORTEPIANO The 14th to 16th centuries saw the rise of the harpsichord, a keyboard instrument whose characteristic tinkling sound is produced by plucking, not striking, the strings. In 1709 Bartolomeo Cristofori constructed the first fortepiano, which offered the performer the new ability to vary the volume and duration of a tone by varying the touch on a key. On the piano, the sound is produced by vibrating strings struck by felt hammers that are controlled by the keyboard. Mozart was one of the first great composers to write music for this new instrument. He was also one of its virtuoso performers.

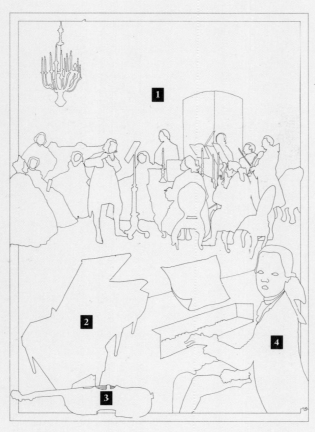

3 THE VIRTUOSO VIOLIN The violin is the ideal virtuoso instrument, and the one that most imitates the human voice. Mozart enjoyed composing for the violin, especially after 1775.

4 BOY WONDER Here is Wolfgang Amadeus Mozart, age twelve, who has just composed six piano sonatas for the queen of England. He was composing music before he could write the alphabet. At the age of six, he and his twelve-year-old sister performed for the Elector of Bavaria and then for Empress Maria Theresa in Vienna. Mozart traveled constantly throughout his brief life. He was born in 1756, in Salzburg, Austria, about 150 miles west of Vienna, and died in Vienna in December 1791 while working on his sublime *Requiem*. His sister-in-law, Sophie, who was at his deathbed, said, "His last movement was an attempt to express with his mouth a drum passage in the *Requiem*. I can hear it still."

London, 19th century

Contemporary life as most city dwellers know it today first took shape in 19th-century London. Indoor plumbing, streetlights, and plate-glass shop windows; buses, taxis, and trains to the suburbs; traffic jams and air pollution—these were certainly not unique to London, but they existed there on a scale that was unknown elsewhere.

Writers rushed to describe and explain and judge the spectacle of this extraordinary place. The poet Percy Bysshe Shelley said, "Hell is a city much like London—A populous and a smoky city." The novelist Henry James was enthusiastic: "It is not a pleasant place . . . it is only magnificent," he wrote, and added, "It is the biggest aggregation of human life—the most complete compendium of the world." By and large, Londoners themselves were proud of the behemoth they had created.

"Biggest" hardly did it justice, for 19th-century England introduced into human life a new way to measure growth, by multiplying rather than adding. If the new machines that powered the Industrial Revolution could multiply the amount of goods the economy produced, they also seemed to multiply the rest of life in a bewildering manner: the speed of travel, the numbers of the poor, the things to do, the styles of fashion, the crimes committed—an endless list. They even multiplied Greater London itself, which began the century as the world's only "million city" and grew to almost 5 million people at its end.

A GEORGE STEPHENSON'S ROCKET The steam engine changed England and the world in the 19th century. Used to run textile mills and operate cranes and other machinery since the late 18th century, it was soon adapted to power vehicles. One important early locomotive builder was engineer George Stephenson, who helped establish the first passenger-carrying railroad in the world in 1825. His locomotive Rocket won a famous contest in 1829 and was used subsequently by the Liverpool and Manchester Railway. By 1900, there were about 22,000 route miles of track in England, and London was the hub of a dense network of intercity lines.

1 ST. GEORGE'S HALL, LIVERPOOL In the 19th century, Liverpool became England's most important Atlantic seaport and grew at a dramatic rate. St. George's Hall, one of England's finest Greek Revival buildings, completed in 1847, is a monument of those prosperous times.

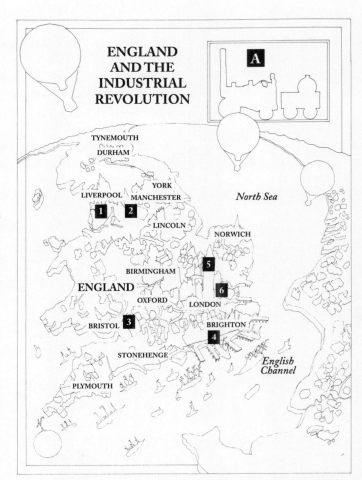

ENGLAND AND THE INDUSTRIAL REVOLUTION

people were killed as a mass protest by workers was dispersed. The taller Gothic Revival Town Hall, completed in 1876, is the city's most prominent building.

3 BANK OF ENGLAND, BRISTOL Bristol was England's main Atlantic seaport until Liverpool overshadowed it. Banks were an important source of capital in the Industrial Revolution.

4 ROYAL PAVILION, BRIGHTON Brighton, southern England's most celebrated seaside resort, was gradually transformed from a fishing village to a fashionable watering spot beginning in the late 18th century, when the Prince of Wales moved into a palace he built there. The palace took its final exotic form—mixing Indian, Chinese, and Gothic influences with happy abandon—by 1822.

5 HOUSES OF PARLIAMENT, LONDON Parliament met in a much rebuilt palace on this site until 1834, when it burned to the ground. Handsome new Gothic Revival buildings were erected by 1860, including the tower with the clock known throughout the world as Big Ben, although strictly speaking the name belongs to the clock's hour bell.

6 ST. PANCRAS STATION, LONDON Here, the great intercity railroad stations of the capitol are represented by St. Pancras (1864), terminus then of the London Midland Railway.

2 FREE TRADE HALL AND TOWN HALL, MANCHESTER American cotton that landed in Liverpool was destined for the textile mills of Lancashire, which were scattered in and around the industrial city of Manchester. There, the first mill to be operated with steam power was established in 1783. In Manchester, the Industrial Revolution generated conflict, hardship, and prosperity. The Free Trade Hall (1856) stands on the site of the 1819 "Peterloo Massacre," in which eleven

Victorian England

1804
EMPEROR
Napoleon I crowned

1810
HAWAII
United by
Kamehameha I

1814
ALL ABOARD!
Stephenson's
first locomo-
tive

1816
ZULU
WARRIOR
Shaka
becomes chief

1831
EVOLUTION
Darwin sails on
the *Beagle*

1833
AND THE
WINNER IS . . .
Alfred Nobel
born

1839
OPIUM WAR
Britain vs.
China

1854
PORTS OPEN
American-
Japanese
treaty

The Flood of Humanity

Not only were there more Londoners than anyone ever imagined possible, but there were more types of them, distinguished from one another in thousands of ways that signified their precise position in the pecking order of society, from the hats on their heads to the food in their stomachs. In the middle of the century, the journalist Henry Mayhew carefully observed and described the city's working people, from such skilled tradesmen as tailors and milliners, shoemakers, cabinetmakers, and carpenters, to men who braved sewer rats to prospect for coins beneath the city's streets.

1865
HEREDITY
EXPLAINED
By Gregor
Mendel

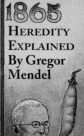

1876
CUSTER'S
LAST STAND
Sioux defeat
U.S. Army

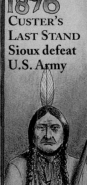

1877
MUSIC BOX
Edison's
phonograph

1895
FIRST NOBEL
WINNER
Wilhelm Roentgen
discovers X rays

1886
MONUMENTAL
GIFT
Statue of Liberty
dedicated

GAZETTE
THIRD EDITION
A.G. AMONG THE MISTS
A BARONESS BEQUEATHS
£250,000 TO CHARITIES
Death of a Famous Actor
THE WHITECHAPEL
MURDER
HEAVY FAILURE AT N.Y.

1 LONDON PEOPLE In this view, some familiar landmarks are visible—among them, Tower Bridge (1886–94) and St. Paul's Cathedral (1675–1708)—but the foreground is designed to be a stage set for the people of London. On the left you can see a suggestion of the bustling docks that once stretched for miles along the River Thames east of the Tower Bridge. On the right, a cross-section of a building reveals Dickensian scenes of London life. Center stage is a typical Victorian street, jammed with carriages and foot traffic.

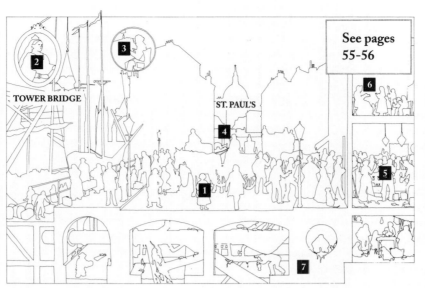

See pages 55-56

TOWER BRIDGE

ST. PAUL'S

4 COMMUTING With the rise of the railroad, the London middle classes began to move to the suburbs. Until about 1850, the railroad was primarily used for travel between cities. Soon, however, it became a daily experience for immense numbers of people. Thousands of houses were destroyed to build lines into the city, but by the century's end even the working man could avail himself of a small house outside of town.

2 QUEEN VICTORIA The queen of England from her accession to the throne in 1837 at the age of eighteen to her death in 1901, Victoria gave her name to an era. She eventually became an enormously popular monarch, whose moral character and devotion to duty perfectly suited the nation's mood. She was associated with three festive pageants in London: the Crystal Palace Exhibition of 1851, masterminded by her consort Prince Albert and visited by her majesty forty-two times; the Golden Jubilee of 1887, celebrating the fiftieth year of her reign; and the Diamond Jubilee ten years later.

3 CHARLES DICKENS (1812–1870) This writer's novels are so strongly evocative of his city that the phrase "Dickensian London" resonates almost as widely as "Victorian London." To Dickens, the human types of London were as easy to categorize as buildings are to an architectural historian, and readers loved his sharp characterizations.

5 PUB The English pub emerged in the 19th century as a neighborhood bar for workingmen, and in turn gave rise to the music hall, as publicans (pub owners) made space available to motley assortments of singers, magicians, dancers, and other would-be entertainers.

6 RAGGED SCHOOL In the 1840s, reformers established schools for the poor, but children were too valuable as labor to keep in school. In the poor neighborhood of East London, most children left school at age ten in 1845. The Education Act of 1870 made elementary education compulsory, and hundreds of Board schools, as they were called, were built.

7 UNDERGROUND Before they were built upwards, industrial cities expanded underground, where there was soon a maze of sewers that contaminated the public water supply, and windowless, overcrowded lodgings, caused by a lack of housing for the poor. London was the first great city to face such social problems on a massive scale, and the first to begin to confront them effectively.

This page shows some of the great variety of dress to be found in London over the course of the century. It is drawn with a humorous and satirical eye.

1 HATS Just about everyone wore a hat when out-of-doors.

2 SWELLS Fashionable young men wore side-whiskers and what a magazine of the day called "an appendage of hair called a mustachio." One of Dickens's characters in *Bleak House* (1852) "quite scented the dining-room with bear's grease and other perfumery." After midcentury, men's clothing became more sedate.

3 DRESSED FOR AN OUTING Victorian men of substance liked heavy materials and a solidly wealthy look. A colored cravat or vest was acceptable.

4 MATCH BOY

5 BUSTLE Skirts grew fuller and fuller until about 1860. One writer described a lady's attire in 1856: "long lace-trimmed drawers, an under petticoat three and a half yards wide, a petticoat wadded at the knees and stiffened in the upper part with whalebone, a white starched petticoat with three stiffly starched flounces, a muslin petticoat, and finally the

dress." Around 1870, the bustle, a whalebone half cage that supported the fullness at the back of the skirt, was introduced. Finally, in the 1890s, skirts began to fall naturally.

6 YEOMEN OF THE GUARD The king's bodyguards last accompanied a monarch on the battlefield in 1743, but they continued to serve a ceremonial function. Their uniforms derived from the 15th century.

7 NEWSPAPER SELLER

8 STUDENT At about age six, a boy would graduate from a skirt to breeches buttoned at the knee.

9 POLICEMAN The Metropolitan Police was created in 1829. Blue was finally chosen for its uniforms to avoid association with the army's redcoats, who were resented in some neighborhoods.

10 FLOWER-SELLERS The life of the London flower seller was inevitably romanticized by George Bernard Shaw in his play *Pygmalion*, and even more so in the musical based on it, *My Fair Lady*.

11 CHIMNEY SWEEP

New York City, 20th Century

In 1524, when Giovanni da Verrazano—another European in search of a route to the Indies—made his way into New York Harbor, he found "a very agreeable site." Indeed, with its natural harbor and easily navigable waterways, New York soon became the world's busiest port, and the prosperous settlement of New Amsterdam (officially founded in 1626, when the Dutch bought the island of Manhattan from the Canarsie Indians for the equivalent of $24) eventually became a huge, crowded city.

Perhaps the most modern of all cities, New York is a constantly changing brew: an Italian neighborhood becomes Chinese; a favorite restaurant is replaced by a new store in the blink of an eye; a skyscraper grows in the hole where an apartment house once took root. It's with good reason that the city is known for its high level of energy, constant growth, and hectic pace.

While it's famous for its museums, performing arts, and restaurants, in many industries—from publishing to banking—New York City remains "the" place to do business. Where the 17th-century Dutch prospered by dealing in beaver, mink, and otter skins, today a vast array of other commodities are produced, bought, and sold. As the turn of a new century approaches, the city remains true to its origins as a commercial capital.

A THE BOROUGHS New York City is made of five boroughs—Manhattan, Brooklyn, Queens, Bronx, and Staten Island—which in 1898 came together to form the most densely populated city in the country at the time. All boroughs but the Bronx are on islands, which can cause formidable challenges to quick transportation. The city is linked by bridges and tunnels perpetually crowded with cars, buses, subways, and trains; ferries parade across the water; and trams and helicopters zip by overhead. Manhattan is known as "The City" to residents of the other boroughs.

1 WORLD TRADE CENTER At 1,350 feet, the World Trade Center—composed of two twin towers—was briefly the tallest building in the world. (It quickly lost the title to Chicago's Sears Tower.) It takes just under a minute for an elevator to reach the top.

2 LOWER EAST SIDE Best known as the traditional home to Eastern European immigrants, today this neighborhood is populated by people from a remarkable mix of ethnic backgrounds.

3 LITTLE ITALY In the 1930s almost every resident of this district was of Italian extraction, but now Manhattan's booming Chinatown is changing traditional neighborhood borders.

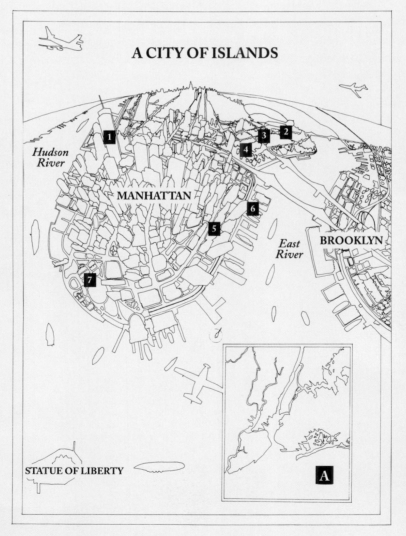

A CITY OF ISLANDS

4 CHINATOWN This busy and crowded neighborhood is filled with wave after wave of immigrants from many parts of Asia, especially Hong Kong. Streets are lined with markets and shops offering a tremendous variety of fish, produce, and other wares.

5 WALL STREET The street itself is just a few blocks long, but the financial district it represents is home to the American and the New York Stock Exchanges, commodity exchanges, and many law firms and banks. The name comes from a wall the Dutch built there in 1653 to protect their settlement from assault.

6 SOUTH STREET SEAPORT This is one of the few places in Manhattan where the city's maritime heritage has been preserved. A museum and a variety of old ships convey the feeling of the past, while shops and restaurants offer more modern pleasures. The Fulton Fish Market has been in operation there since the 18th century.

7 BATTERY PARK On the south tip of Manhattan, this park offers superb views of New York Harbor, including the Statue of Liberty, Ellis Island, and Staten Island. The Staten Island ferry docks just to the east.

A BUSTLING METROPOLIS

1903
TAKE OFF
The Wright
brothers fly a
power-driven
airplane

1905
THEORY OF
RELATIVITY
Presented by
Albert
Einstein

1996
CENTENNIAL
Modern
Olympic Games

1990
FREE AT LAST
Nelson Mandela
released from
prison

1989
BERLIN WALL FALLS
East and West
Germany
unified

1973
NEW OPERA
HOUSE
Opens in
Sydney

1969
ONE SMALL
STEP . . .
Americans
land on the
moon

ORDERED CHAOS

The grid pattern city planners imposed on the young city in 1811 is obvious in midtown Manhattan. Avenues run north and south, and streets go east and west: it's not possible to get hopelessly lost. (These sky-scraper-flanked blocks can, however, be uncomfortably windy when gusts are funneled into these urban canyons.) New York is less the proverbial melting pot than a kaleidoscope of cultures. The more than eighty languages spoken in the city reflect the national origins of its diverse population. The city is in a constant state of ethnic flux.

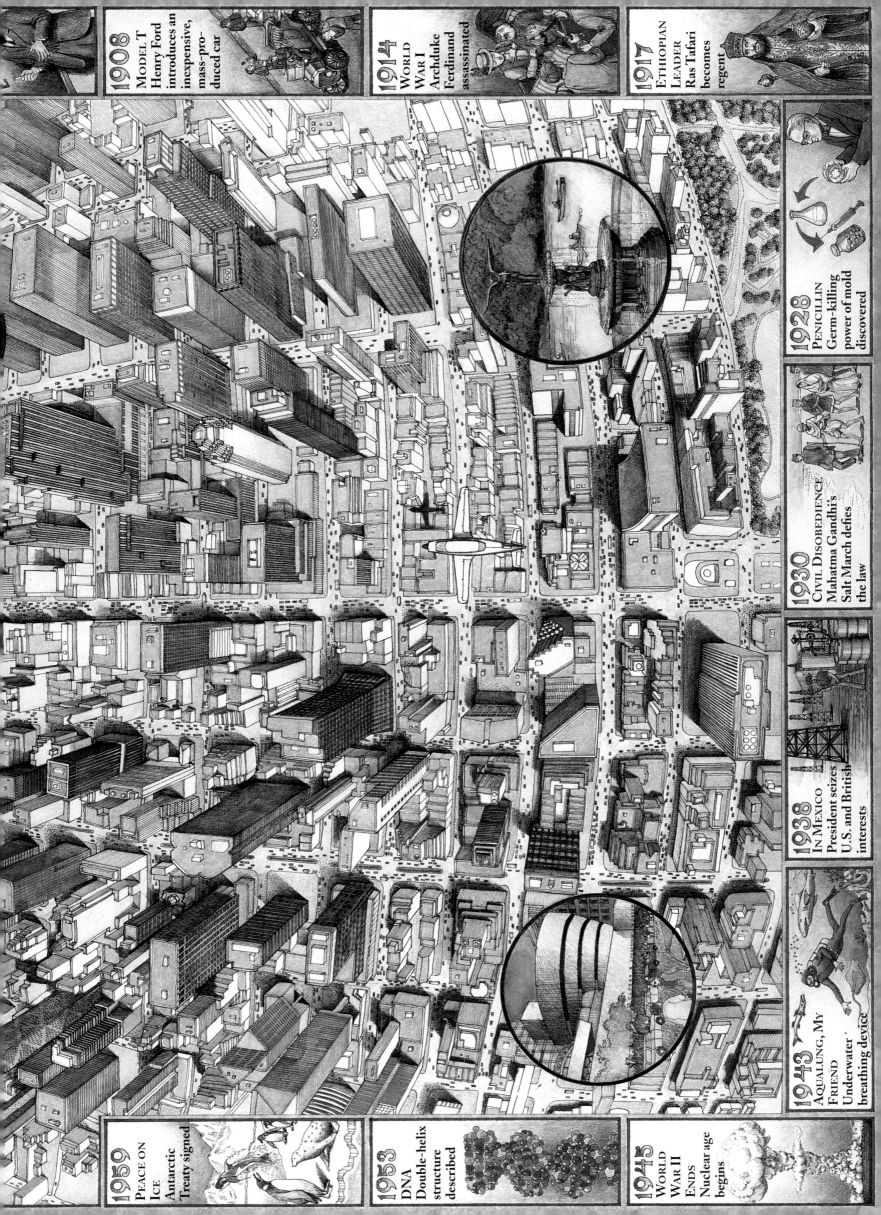

1908
MODEL T
Henry Ford introduces an inexpensive, mass-produced car

1914
WORLD WAR I
Archduke Ferdinand assassinated

1917
ETHIOPIAN LEADER
Ras Tafari becomes regent

1928
PENICILLIN
Germ-killing power of mold discovered

1930
CIVIL DISOBEDIENCE
Mahatma Gandhi's Salt March defies the law

1938
IN MEXICO
President seizes U.S. and British interests

1943
AQUALUNG, MY FRIEND
Underwater breathing device

1945
WORLD WAR II ENDS
Nuclear age begins

1953
DNA
Double-helix structure described

1959
PEACE ON ICE
Antarctic Treaty signed

1 UNITED NATIONS In 1945 World War II ended, and the United Nations was formed "to save succeeding generations from the scourge of war." The headquarters were built on a parcel of land by the East River between 42nd and 48th streets.

2 EMPIRE STATE BUILDING Rising high above the corner of Fifth Avenue and 34th Street, this building was the tallest in the world until the World Trade Center stole the title. Originally, giant airships were to dock on its tower. When it opened in 1931, the "Empty State Building" was more than 50 percent vacant. It costarred in the 1933 movie *King Kong*.

3 STATUE OF LIBERTY In 1886 France presented this statue, which has become a universal symbol of freedom, to the United States. One Frenchman who helped conceive this monument said, "This will be . . . the American Liberty, who brandishes not an incendiary torch, but the one that lights the way." An elevator takes visitors to the top of the pedestal, and then a spiral staircase leads to the crown.

4 TIMES SQUARE The Theater District comprises the area around this famous intersection of Broadway and Seventh Avenue, not really a square at all.

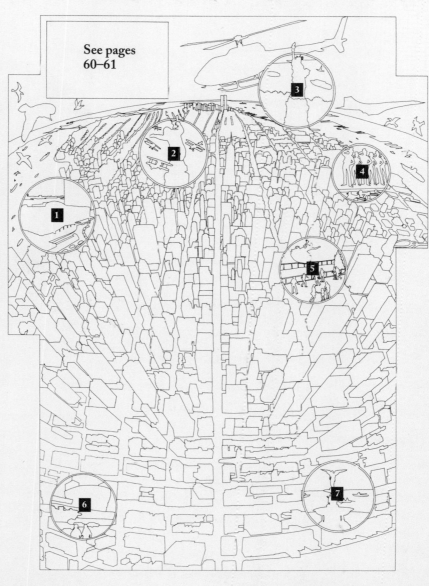

See pages 60–61

5 ROCKEFELLER CENTER One writer has said that this complex "embodies [New York's] essence, trumpets its pride in the same way that the solemn splendor of cathedrals symbolized the very essence of urban communities in the Middle Ages." Including fourteen buildings built in the 1930s plus another five completed after 1945, this was Manhattan's largest building project at the time. The skating rink is a popular winter attraction.

6 GUGGENHEIM MUSEUM In 1943 wealthy copper magnate and modern art collector Solomon Guggenheim commissioned noted architect Frank Lloyd Wright to design a museum that would be unlike any other in New York. The scheme Wright designed followed a 1,416-foot-long spiral ramp gradually climbing to a glass dome that illuminates the entire building with natural light.

7 CENTRAL PARK At first, city planners neglected to include a park in their thinking, but this was corrected in the mid-1800s, much to the gratitude of future generations of New Yorkers, who look to the 840 acres of meadows, lakes, bridges, trails, ball fields, and just plain open space—such a rare commodity in New York—as a haven of peace and relaxation.

New Yorkers love to eat, and every bit of their heritage gets stirred into the mix. Here is a sampling of what's on New York City's bountiful and varied menu every day of the week:

1 A TASTE OF THE CARIBBEAN Exotic fruit, hot sauce, fish, sugarcane

2 AN ITALIAN FEAST Pasta, bread, pizza, wine, espresso

3 RUSSIAN/UKRAINIAN/BALTIC FOOD Blinis with sour cream and caviar, pierogi, borscht, chicken Kiev

4 GERMAN SAUSAGES AND BEER From bologna to braunschweiger

5 GREEK/MIDDLE EASTERN TREATS Souvlaki, stuffed grape leaves

6 MEXICAN FIESTA Tamales, enchiladas, frijoles, guacamole, tortilla chips and salsa, jalapeños rellenos, flan

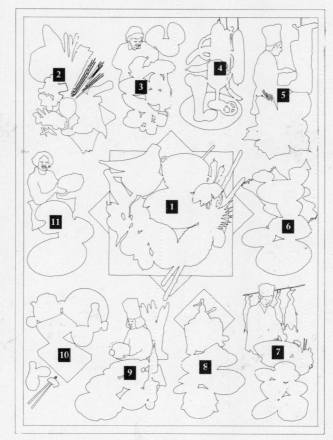

7 CHINESE RESTAURANT Wonton soup, steamed dumplings, roast duck, cold noodles and sesame sauce, fried shrimp, broccoli with minced ham, stir-fried chicken, rice

8 JEWISH DELI Bagel and lox, matzoball soup, corned beef on rye, chocolate egg cream, cheesecake, mandelbrot, hamantaschen

9 THE FRENCH INFLUENCE Quiche, seafood mousse, baguettes, crêpes, a variety of fine pastries, liqueur, chocolate soufflé

10 JAPANESE SUSHI BAR Sushi with ginger and soy sauce, clear soup with tofu, green tea, sake

11 FOOD FOR THE SOUL: SOUTHERN REGIONAL COOKING Fried chicken, barbecued ribs, corn bread, collard greens, black-eyed peas, sweet-potato pie

For our families

Acknowledgments

I would like to thank the following members of my studio for their diligence and creative assistance over the past two years. Neil Mahimtura, Dickson Leung, Myron Mirgorodsky, and Gonzalo Bustamante were especially invaluable to the production of this book. Ilya Mirgorodsky, John Perkins, Wendy Kui, Yin Wai Teh, Po Shan Lee, and Meghan Corwin were also tremendously helpful.

Thanks are also due to my editor, Eric Himmel, for his guidance, constructive criticism, and constancy; Sharon AvRutick, who transformed my inconsistent, rambling descriptions into a professional and readable text; and Darilyn Lowe Carnes, for constructing a well-designed book.

Finally, my gratitude to my wife, Maureen. Without her, this whole project would still be hibernating in a cave.

PROJECT MANAGER: *Eric Himmel*
EDITOR: *Sharon AvRutick*
DESIGNER: *Darilyn Lowe Carnes*

Library of Congress Catalog Card Number: 96–83709
ISBN 0–8109–4284–4

Published in 1996 by Harry N. Abrams, Incorporated, New York
A Times Mirror Company

Printed and bound in Hong Kong